THE TR

Rowan Williams s
College, Cambridge, and at Wadham College,
Oxford, where he wrote his thesis on modern
Russian Orthodox theology. He spent two years
at the theological college at Mirfield, before
becoming Chaplain and Tutor at Westcott House,
Cambridge in 1977.

Since 1980 he has been Lecturer in Divinity,
University of Cambridge, and a Canon Theologian of Leicester Cathedral.

Rowan Williams is the author of *The Wound of
Knowledge* and *Resurrection*, both published by
Darton, Longman & Todd.

The Archbishop of Canterbury's
Lent Books

*Previous titles published by
Fount Paperbacks,
in association with Faith Press*

THE WAY OF A DISCIPLE   George Appleton
SQUARE WORDS IN A ROUND WORLD   Eric Kemp
PILGRIMAGE AND PROMISE   Michael Marshall
BE STILL AND KNOW   Michael Ramsey

Rowan Williams

THE TRUCE
OF GOD

With a Foreword by the
Archbishop of Canterbury

Collins
FOUNT PAPERBACKS
in association with Faith Press

First published by Fount Paperbacks, London,
in association with Faith Press, in 1983

© Rowan Williams 1983

Made and printed in Great Britain by
William Collins Sons & Co Ltd, Glasgow

CONTENTS

FOREWORD

Nobody would deny that the search for peace in the world is one of mankind's most important tasks. Our Lord said 'Blessed are the peace makers' and his followers cannot justify the name of Christian unless they share his passion for peace.

The subject, however, is commonly overlaid with bland consensus clichés and the kind of pious rhetoric which has a bewildering and depressing effect even upon the best-intentioned. The merit of Rowan Williams' new book *The Truce of God* is that it probes behind words like 'reconciliation' which we use too easily, to reveal the profound realism of the way in which the concepts of peace and violence have been understood in the Bible and in later Christian tradition.

Although the author is a distinguished young theologian working in a university, his book is not academic in the pejorative sense. It is fresh and contemporary in its language and illustrations, and organized in such a way that it would provide an excellent and creatively controversial basis for a Lent study group.

The Truce of God is an enemy to easy illusions and a sign that the Christian faith has the potential to make a unique contribution to peace making. I hope that it will be widely studied.

Lambeth Palace
November 1982

Robert Cantuar:

INTRODUCTION

Anyone picking up a Lent Book and finding its opening pages mostly concerned with the world of popular fantasy and fiction might be forgiven for feeling some bewilderment; so a brief word of explanation may be in order. When I was invited to begin work on this book, I felt an urgent need to move away a little from the normal patterns of this sort of literature and see what it might be like to approach questions about Christian life and prayer in the context of a highly specific set of contemporary concerns – asking, in effect, what is the good news for *this* situation?

Such an approach is full of potential pitfalls. You can so define the 'contemporary concerns' that the Gospel fits neatly into the place you have already cleared for it; you can trivialize the Gospel by binding it to the passing trends of secular interest. I expect this book will be accused of both failings, and I am aware that it is unlikely to have avoided these traps entirely. But I cannot believe that the effort is misplaced. An essay in Christian spirituality written in the 1980s which completely ignored the collective neuroses of our society would be dishonest and destructive: it would imply that 'spirituality' was *not* about the learning of a particular kind of human life, open-eyed, responsive and candid. And because a great part of our collective neurosis seems to me to be rooted in certain sorts of fear, with their consequent refusal to *see*, I have chosen to come at the question of what it is like now to live and pray Christianly by way of looking at our fears and their slow corruption of our imagination. So that the goal of a book like this one is something to do with a salutary shock to the imagination and a rebirth of its proper critical and hopeful dimensions.

I have written about peace, internal and external. I make no secret of the fact that I have strong convictions about the way forward to a more peaceful and less threatened world, convictions which I hold in common with a growing number of Christian people, including the authors of the Anglican report on *The Church and the Bomb*, which appeared when this book was at proof stage. Obviously I run the risk of having this volume dismissed as partisan or propagandist by those who think that any expression of opinion on this subject by Christians is some sort of compromising of the non-political purity of the Gospel. But it is not meant as a propaganda exercise on behalf of one kind of political solution. Many will disagree with my response to the problem: my hope, though, is that some agreement may be possible about the *nature* of the problem and its theological and spiritual dimensions. With this in mind, I have tried to concentrate on this latter area rather than on the vexed questions of practical policy making.

A lot of what I have written owes a great debt to the work of Thomas Merton, and I can say that this book is, in some sense, written in his honour and for his memory. But I have also to acknowledge all those living friends and teachers who have shared their wisdom with me – Professor Donald Mackinnon above all, and many Christian acquaintances in Cambridge over the past few years: Jim Garrison, Roger Paul, Alan Smith, Peter Tamplin, and others engaged in the cause of peace and in discussing the Christian issues involved. This book would be duller and shallower without them. And lastly, my warm thanks to the Archbishop of Canterbury for encouraging the writing of this work and for providing a foreword: his generous support has helped enormously.

R.W.

CHAPTER 1

FEARS AND FANTASIES

There is no shortage of people to complain that ours is a society obsessed with violence. But by 'violence', such people usually mean not much more than the level of realism with which physical struggle and physical injury are shown on television and cinema screens; analysis of the context and the character of this surface violence seems less forthcoming. Yet it is an analysis badly needed. There is nothing much new about the realities of struggle and injury, and long before an advanced special effects technology made film representation of this so much more appallingly convincing, explicit verbal description was perfectly possible and not at all rare. It may well be that the level of realism we now tolerate in visual representations of violence means that our imaginations are becoming significantly brutalized or insensitive: I think this is probably so, and it is worrying, but it isn't the main point I want to make at the moment.

What is new, and what does need analysis, is the kind of violence which seems to have swamped enormous areas of the popular market, especially in the cinema and in cheap paperback fiction. It is not easy to characterize it in a nutshell; but I suppose its main feature could be seen as a quality of utter uncontrollability and unpredictability quite removed from the human scale and from the sphere of normal human interaction. One form of this is the 'catastrophe' fantasy based on the malfunctioning or collapse of some bit of the rather threatening world of complex technology – the aircraft disaster, the burning tower block, the chemical leak. Out of the vague sense most of us have, that in a sophisticated technology there are countless things that just might go wrong on an enormous scale, fantasy generates the details for a disaster story. And perhaps the most important aspect of this process is the recognition that, in a technologically advanced society, most people are powerless to remedy errors or avoid fatal breakdown because of their ignorance. The specialized knowledge required to understand the electrical wiring of a large block of flats – to take only the most simple instance – is not available to most of us. It is made to work for us by those who know; it is not something we are aware of doing or making, not something for which we have any sense of responsibility. So if it should go wrong, producing disaster, pain, death, this is something done *to* us. Uncontrollable force has been unleashed against us, and we are helpless victims.

This is a fairly obvious reading of a fairly obvious fantasy – which of us has not had at least moments of stomach-turning anxiety in an aeroplane, the sense of tempting fate by doing something so complicated as flying? We can afford to take the 'disaster' novel or film with an embarrassed laugh, admitting its uncomfortable accuracy about our humiliating neuroses. But as a phenomenon side by side with others of similar kind, it may look rather more disturbing. The first cousin of the *Towering Inferno* fantasy is the *Exorcist* fantasy. Deeper and more irrational dread is involved here: what if the world is populated by powerful, hostile, more-or-less-personal forces that we can't see, hear or touch and have no recognized means of dealing with? They can see us, they are stronger than we, and they work in ways of which we have practically no knowledge. Here again, the violence involved in fantasies of the occult or paranormal is what is done *to* us, it is force unleashed against us. The power to hurt and destroy is alienated from human possession and transferred to other agencies, and so it becomes uncontrollable. And of course in a secular society, which has no tradition of 'skills' in dealing with, interpreting or resisting the paranormal, it is easy to understand why this is a field in which extreme and neurotic fear has free play.

A major image here is that of the possessed child. The one who is both victim and point of entry for diabolical force is someone who is not an adult and not precisely a full member of society. And this seems to represent a blurring of two different sorts of perception. On the other hand, children (even teenagers) can stand for innocence and vulnerability: as victims of the alien power, they can be images for ourselves, equally innocent, equally vulnerable. Yet they are also the agents of the devil; some writers have pointedly observed that the fantasy of one's children being 'possessed' is one congenial to a generation of parents faced with incomprehensible rebellion from their children. There can be no 'reason' for revolt; and so it is tempting to think of it as imposed upon them. They are being manipulated unawares by invisible enemies of immense resourcefulness and subtlety . . .

That is a theme we shall have to come back to. But it is at this point that the 'paranormal' fantasy begins to shade into the closely related one of insane violence – the psychopathic mass murderer who waits in the back streets of cities, in isolated rural districts, on the edges of the youth camp, and so on. He (the masculine pronoun is deliberate) is again specially interested in the vulnerable and the marginal, and is a particular threat to the lone woman (the number of recent films involving pathological violence against women is striking). In this area, it is not so much a matter of violence done to *us*; there is a much stronger voyeuristic element, especially for the reader or viewer who is not young, female or alone. But the violence still has the same curiously amoral quality, it is done by an agent outside the ordinary range of social control and reasoned decision. The violence of a psychopath is not all that far removed from a natural disaster – or from the 'violence' of an animal.

So this kind of fantasy relates closely to a final category in which the human element is almost entirely removed – imaginings of uncontrollable animal attack, by sharks, wolves, rats, and other natural villains of the animal world. These vary from the fairly naturalistic (like the immortal *Jaws*) to the wildly implausible (the giant ape/prehistoric monster family of fictions). Somewhere in between lie stories of unimaginably huge plagues of beasts or birds, multiplied in number and in strength (even increased in size) by some chance development – perhaps a technological slip, which would neatly combine this with our first category. Science fiction in the narrower sense can reflect the same concerns, and articulate once more the feeling that things are too complex: we have intruded upon areas where we should not go, because we do not know enough to deal with what we might meet. Nature will be revenged on our presumption. That highly imaginative space fantasy, *Alien*, managed to combine all this with something rather like the 'possession' theme. There may, then, be a vague sense of culpability in this sort of fiction, yet it is badly focused: guilt about 'interfering with nature' is an ambiguous thing, since no one (quite rightly) is able to say that this is a matter of simple or self-evident good and evil. The 'Faustian' worry – have we gone too far? – is an uneasiness in which it is hard to disentangle real moral concern from the mere dread of increased responsibility.

The family resemblances between all these types of fantasy have to do with the source and nature of violence:

all of them clearly reflect the sense that violence is something done *to* us by agencies over which we have no control. It isn't even a question of apportioning 'guilt' for violence to someone else: the agents of it are beyond or below moral assessment. Violence 'happens'. Without real human causes, without roots, without a history, tremendous destructive energies surge up to mutilate and kill. In a sense, they cannot help it any more than we can; psychopaths, animals, natural or supernatural forces simply obey their own inner laws. And the conclusion that is implied in all this is that violence is never something ordinary human beings *decide to do*.

I think this implication is still there in the way these fantasies deal with people's reactions to the unpredictable attacks made on them. There certainly are reactions, counter-measures are taken, and often they are bloody and extreme. Those thought to be 'possessed', for example, can be tied up, beaten, deprived, and so on (which is of course just how such people have so often been treated in our history); animals can be mutilated and killed. It sounds violent enough; but because it is legitimate and unavoidable defence, it will not count as 'real' violence. As a natural and instinctive reaction, it is rather like the attack which provokes it in having very little to do with choice and morality. Extreme circumstances dictate harsh and dramatic responses.

So if we try to feel our way towards a general sense of what the contemporary fantasy world is telling us about violence and destruction, the result seems to be this: pain and injury and sudden death are unpredictable, not planned or chosen by anyone like ourselves, yet always threatening, always around the corner. Against this threat, we defend ourselves as the situation dictates – without many qualms about how we do so, because we are not dealing with agents like ourselves, whose motives and methods would need scrutiny, about whom we might be able to make considered predictions. Violence does not belong in the moral world; it has nothing to do with human responsibility, with the kinds of choices by which we make up our lives from day to day. You could almost say that it is a non-human phenomenon, in the sense that it is so strange and specialized a happening. And it always begins 'somewhere else' – in the mysterious and uncontrollable world Out There.

*

A society's mass fantasies are anything but trivial, and I do not think we have anything to gain by underrating or simply mocking them. It is all very well to say that nobody with a grain of intelligence 'takes these things seriously'. But what does it mean to 'take them seriously'? Granted that people do not, on the whole, *believe* that they are going to be devoured by plagues of giant rats, possessed by demons as arbitrarily as they might catch a cold, invaded by parasites from outer space, and so on, why are these images so magnetic? Why do even those who, in the cold light of day, would laugh off such things, provide the public for them? There may be nothing very new in some of the themes of such fantasy (H.G. Wells anticipated quite a lot of them), but, if the station bookstall and the cinema are anything to go by, they are now more dominant and compulsive images than they have been. Societies give themselves away in their favourite fantasies; they betray their assumptions about what the world is really like. And that is a very good reason for taking popular fantasy with a great deal of seriousness.

On the basis of what we have looked at so far, it certainly seems as though our society is aware of enormous but badly-defined threats – some internal (arising from the complications of technology), but most external. It is, as a result, tense and afraid, and alarmingly confused because it cannot locate the real sources of danger. More disturbingly, though, it is incapable of seeing this as a *moral* problem – as something to do with power, vision, understanding and choice, with the ways in which we decide to make sense of our lives. And it is incapable of turning a critical eye on itself, asking how far the condition of chronic insecurity it experiences has roots in its own preferences and options. Instead, it chooses to see itself as innocent and vulnerable, recognizing that the world is full of destructive potential, but refusing to deal with this recognition in human moral terms.

It is a kind of fatalism; but as we have noted already, it leaves room for defensive action, which does not in any way diminish our innocence. If we do not and cannot ask about the origins of our experience of a threat of destructive violence, our reactions can only be dictated by that present experience. The situation alone will justify how we act, because analysis and longer perspective are more or less impossible. Long-range calculation about the effects of our 'defensive action' is not the most important thing, because in a fatalistic world it is impossible to see how the situation might escalate.

Thus the picture suggested is – depressingly – one of a society in full flight from the notion of responsibility. Unfortunately, the phrase 'responsible society' has recently been effectively kidnapped by one particular interest group; so I must make it clear that in using language about 'responsible societies' I mean to refer to societies capable of seeing themselves critically and of acting and planning and organizing themselves with some degree of conscious awareness. I also have in mind societies with a sense of history – i.e. societies which can understand how they came to be what they are. This is a necessary part of understanding how societies are created *now*.

But this does not encourage us to see our society (and by 'our' I mean the European-North Atlantic world as a whole) as responsible. Instead it appears as frightened, obstinate, self-pitying, self-righteous and wilfully short-sighted. If an individual presented that kind of image, we should with reason worry about his or her mental health. A Christian would say that such a person is in spiritual danger because of an inability to 'repent': if you cannot both recognize and criticize your own actions as yours, you are trapped in an egoism which repels all real nourishment, all real love or grace, from outside itself. If this is so, ours is an 'impenitent' society – not in the sense that word often suggests, of someone bold and hardened in crime, but because it is too terrified to open its eyes to the truth.

What, then, are the grounds for such stubborn fear? What produces a mentality so desperately eager to avoid guilt? If it were impossible to find anything in the real world which would explain this, we might have to think again about the significance of modern fantasy. But the truth is that there is an almost embarrassingly obvious context into which our fantasies can be fitted. We have been living for several decades with the knowledge that we are at last capable of obliterating the greater part of the human world in war. We know that 'our' societies are technically capable of this, and we also know that 'the others' are also in a position to do it. Grounds enough for a pervasive feeling of being threatened. Because the possession and development of arms of this kind is, on the face of it, morally outrageous, justification has been provided by the notion of 'deterrence': the Other Side must be the aggressor, and we shall never be anything other than the innocent victim, driven to retaliation by the horror of our circumstances.

So far this is a very common strategy indeed. Decide well in advance that others are in the wrong automatically and by definition, and you need never worry about your moral standing. Trollope, in *Barchester Towers*, remarks that 'Wise people, when they are in the wrong, always put themselves right by finding fault with the people against whom they have sinned.' Much of the rhetoric of 'deterrence' in our political thinking conceals the determination to be automatically in the right. We do not really choose to have a nuclear arsenal; we certainly should never choose to use it. But the diabolical greed and aggressiveness of the Other Side compels us to protect ourselves; in a way, it is not truly an act of our own, it does not express what we want.

All the evidence suggests that this is a vehicle offered for the salving of conscience rather than a report of the rather more sophisticated mental processes of military planners and strategists, for whom the problems are much more nakedly concerned with power and dominance. One of the unsettling features of public discussion of war and peace in the last two or three years has been an increasing readiness on the part of politicians not to bother about tender consciences, but to be far more candid about the questions of power and victory. There is certainly less reluctance to admit that we might after all be the first to use nuclear weaponry in an international conflict if things are going badly. The idea of a deterrent as a tragic necessity imposed on an innocent and peace-loving society becomes less and less convincing.

But it is still something most people – in all sincerity – want to cling to. No country today is really content with an image of itself as hungry for power at all costs. So the populations of each nation will still prefer something that enables them to be innocent in their own eyes. Yet this is not all. War, and the preparation for war, has always recommended itself by such means. But total war, with the prospect of more or less universal annihilation, poses still deeper problems for the 'mind' of a society at large. The imagination baulks at the thought of anyone, even the diabolical Other Side, actually desiring a holocaust, thinking the price worth paying – and in this respect the imagination should be congratulated on its weakness (or its common sense, depending on how you look at it). It becomes harder and harder to conceive of what it might be like to *decide* to start a war with risks of this magnitude. And the simple solution is to treat the catastrophe of nuclear war as if it were a natural disaster, both unpredictable and unavoidable.

That is exactly what the majority of people seem to do, even at the conscious level. Opinion polls regularly tell us that startlingly large numbers of people are pretty convinced that there will be a war before the end of the century. In other words, they have stopped believing that possession of a 'deterrent' is really likely to make a difference to the way things will probably turn out, and they have no very great trust in the passionate desire for peace of their own government or its allies. This may be realistic enough; but it also indicates that people do not see their own preferences and decisions as having anything to do with what governments will do.

A frightening prospect, if we look at it honestly: when large portions of a population are effectively convinced that their lives and destinies are out of their control, that is a mentality we normally associate with totalitarianism. Someone else is deciding what will happen to you. And the insecurities of life in these conditions are reflected very clearly in fantasies of threat and disaster. Yet not even in these fantasies do we find the imagination managing to conceive of someone *deciding for* violence and destruction. As we have seen above, in analysing our popular collective nightmares, no one is really to blame for anything.

So the picture becomes darker and darker. Not only do we have the 'totalitarian' mentality, the conviction that nothing we do or want is going to make a difference to our fate; we are also convinced that those whose actions bring about destruction are no more genuinely free than we are. It is not that we fear that those in power will make a foolish or wicked decision: they will be victims like us. Victims of what? It is not easy to say – but people certainly do speculate on the possibility of war being unleashed by some kind of technical accident (a resurgence of the old nightmare of an over-complex technology), or they wonder uneasily about the mental health of the powerful. But it is in any case as if an iron law of ever-growing probability exerted its own compulsion. It will not be chosen, but it will still happen.

Some readers may be feeling by now that I have made far too much of the nature of our fantasies, and that it is itself a fantasy to relate the mentality of *Jaws*, *The Exorcist* or *Alien* to a society threatened by war. Possibly; but I still believe that we should be putting the question of why this particular kind of disaster-fantasy is so prevalent among us. Whatever the exact explanation, it unmistakably reflects fear and powerlessness at once; and few would want to deny that a major incentive for feelings of fear and powerlessness is the menace of total war. What our collective nightmares do for us is not to remove a fear that is perfectly well-grounded, but to reinforce our unwillingness to think about these matters in terms of guilt and responsibility. That is why I decided to begin these reflections by looking at our fantasy life. If these dreams are fulfilling a function for us – and dreams do perform necessary jobs for us in helping us to live with our tensions and conflicts – and that function is chiefly one of confirming our innocence, it is right to be suspicious about what it is in our world that makes it so urgent to avoid the feeling of guilt.

No sane person could actively want to destroy the world, to buy victory at the price of the human race itself; yet this is virtually what is threatened by the conflict of nuclear super-powers. How do we understand such a contradiction? We cope with it, miserably and unconvincingly, by denying implicitly that will and choice have anything to do with it. We assume that we (including our leaders) have no power to change the situation. We behave as if we were not living in 'democratic' societies, where choice and change are essential things, written into the definitions of democracy. With all our public talk about freedom and the 'free world', we appear to be taking it for granted in one basic area that we are not free at all. Public language and experienced reality are hopelessly falling apart. It seems that a very large percentage of our society believes deep down that human beings are not free after all – or rather they choose to believe this, because the alternative is too shocking.

What is this alternative? To believe that we are indeed free, and are capable of freely embarking on courses of action that hurt and destroy. And we embark on such courses not out of a demonic urge towards violence, but because we are unwilling to look critically at what we do, to assess the consequences of what we do, to relate our individual wants to the wider needs of a community – or a world. Comfortable short-sightedness and self-deception produce the worst cruelties; and they produce them by a gradual accumulation of small, hardly noticeable choices of unexamined self-centredness.

In social and political terms this means that we can gradually get ourselves into a position where an elected government is carrying out or condoning atrocities that individuals in the society would find it very hard to say that they wanted to see happening. How many ordinary Germans would have said in the 1930s that they *wanted* institutions like Auschwitz or Maidanek? How many individuals in America in the 1960s would have *wanted* a single Vietnamese child to die – let alone to die by being fatally burned by napalm? Yet at elections political choices had been made which enabled these things to be done – small choices, in a way, choices for parties offering a little more comfort, a better national 'image', so that the morally awkward bits of their programmes could be overlooked for the time being. And so when people wake up to what is being done in their name, they feel able to disown it, because they do not feel they have actively wanted it. And if the government act like this, perhaps it is because they too have no real choice; they cannot actively want to do such things, so there must be good reasons for their doing them, of which we know nothing . . . And so on.

Of course it is a mistake, and a serious one, to over-estimate the power we have to change things in even the most resolutely democratic institutions. But the disowning of responsibility is undoubtedly the mark of a deep sickness of the spirit, struggling to keep pain, horror and destruction away from the sphere of my soul, my desires and hopes. And this sickness, while it appears to be a way of protecting ourselves, in fact prevents us using our spiritual resources to confront and assimilate the pain and guilt we cannot bear.

A psychotherapist*, writing on 'the Bomb as an instrument of mass suicide', has said that the process of 'deadening of feelings and fragmentation of the mind', of

* Dr Nini E. Ettlinger.

neurotic and hopeless flight from reality, is prompted partly by the pace and the scale of catastrophe in this century. We have already – in the World Wars, in the Holocaust, in famine and genocide, and, less drastically, in the destruction of families and environments – seen more devastation than we can easily cope with. We are losing the capacity to 'mourn' – to draw on reserves of compassion that help us to re-affirm values, feeling the enormity of pain and death and violence, and feeling it because we have a richer and better hope for men and women. When there is no time or energy to mourn because there is too much to mourn for, hopelessness takes over, accompanied by the lack of a sense of responsibility. And so, faced with the risk of nuclear annihilation on top of all the other horrors of the last seventy years, it is understandable that such a sickness should prevail.

It is a way of buying a certain kind of 'peace'. It does not do away with fear, but it does at least seem to ease the moral strain. It absolves us from facing the humiliating picture of ourselves as idle, self-indulgent and culpably ignorant, suggested when we take our freedom seriously. We do not have to think about guilt. Yet – as we have already remarked – this means that repentance is not a possibility; and if repentance is impossible, so is grace, reconciliation, hope. So this is a 'peace' which must be unmasked for the lie it is – peace bought at the cost of reality, at the cost of human dignity. Our evasive fantasies must be brought to judgement before we can be brought to grace.

*

In our day more than ever, war and peace are 'spiritual' as well as tactical and political issues. We shall not understand our society and its terrors and anxieties about total war unless we grasp that behind these anxieties lies a profound sickness of spirit; and it is a sickness which only succeeds in reinforcing the structures that give rise to it in the first place.

Gospel, good news, for a society like ours must involve a clear and accurate diagnosis of this kind of sickness, because only so will it become possible to open the doors of repentance once again. Just as in individual therapy it is so important to restore to people the power to mourn, to reawaken both sensitivity and hope, so for society at large war – or rather warlikeness – produces the crippled spirits of totalitarianism. War is to be dreaded (if we can echo the words of Jesus) not so much because it kills the body as because it destroys both body and soul, because its casualties are health and truth and hope. To resist this destruction is to affirm a faith in a human future ; and the Gospel, by driving us to penitence, grounds this affirmation of the future in the loving will of God, remaking us through our conversion.

To be 'converted' means, in this connection, to retrieve the vision of one's own responsibility, and to learn to look in critical openness at one's own life and the shared life of society around. So that conversion is also vocation – the call to *be* free, to take up responsibility and work out how it can be exercised, even in the most apparently unpromising circumstances. We can, of course, make the mistake of thinking that the Gospel prescribes simple answers to the problem of working this out – so that some solutions, which seem obvious to us, are given the authority of the Gospel itself. But the world we live in is a world in which we do not have clear paths open before us; we are not able normally to decide on a simple course of action and carry it through without opposition or the need for adjustment and adaptation. There is a huge difference between recovering a sense of the power to choose and to act in hope, and acquiring a sense of power *over* things, power to shape the world as I want it. And to learn to live with the truth that the latter is an empty illusion is a great part of what we mean by moral maturity.

The Gospel frees us from fear and fantasy, from the nightmares of guilt and insecurity which paralyse our imagination and so prevent us from positive and meaningful action. But precisely because it is the great enemy of self-indulgent fantasy, it frees us into a real world where flexibility and discrimination are vital. I have avoided using the word 'compromise' for this – partly for the simple reason that it is a 'negative' word in most people's minds, and partly because I suspect that there *is* a distinction between a mere readiness to come to a workable arrangement and a sensitivity to the many, often unsatisfactory, means needed to attain a vision or a goal.

So that when we speak about peace and working for peace, I am not sure whether any one programme for peace is uniquely the right one from the Christian standpoint. I write as a passionate believer in unilateral nuclear disarmament, but not as an absolute pacifist (someone who would in all circumstances refuse active participation in a violent conflict); I believe that the practical and moral analyses of both multilateralists and 'absolute pacifists' are hopelessly inadequate. But that disagreement is a matter of continuing discussion and learning, and it is not one I wish to pursue here. What is crucial is that we should be able to share a sense of the outrage to humanity involved in our present situation. A Christian satisfied with this situation, or accepting it as inevitable, would be a very odd kind of Christian. There may be no programme on which we can agree; but we should at least share the conviction that a society menaced by and obsessed with nuclear war is one in need of a clear statement of the good news of liberation – which also involves a proclamation of judgement on all evasions and trivializings of our situation, both inside and outside the Church, and a serious and committed pursuing of the debate about means.

At the moment, there is no peace. The Christian Church would betray its vocation if it pretended there were, 'healing the wound of my people lightly'. The wound needs exposing; we have to call for repentance, for mourning such as we are in danger of forgetting. And we have to struggle for a truer peace. What that peace might mean is what I hope to explore in what follows – looking at the idea of the Church itself as a sign of peace, at the false and cheap images of reconciliation by which we are sometimes tempted, at the implications of talking about *Christ's* peace, and at the subtle interrelations of peace with Christian contemplation and Christian action. Can we preach and live a peace which is a positive and active criticism of the sickness of fatalism and false innocence?

CHAPTER 2

THE TRUCE OF GOD

In the early Middle Ages, the great Burgundian monastery of Cluny sponsored and encouraged an experiment in conciliation among its feudal neighbours – half-civilized landlords in a state of more or less endemic war with each other. The arrangement, known as 'the truce of God', was that all hostilities should be restricted to three days in the week (Monday to Wednesday). Of course, this was never observed for any length of time with much consistency; and in retrospect its mixture of naïve earnestness and cynicism is rather funny (very characteristic of the Church, somehow . . .). But it is more than a comical bit of mediaeval eccentricity. Behind it lay the recognition that for baptized Christians, sharers in the Body of Christ, to be in a state of war with one another was horrible and ridiculous. The mild ludicrousness of the response pales, however, in comparison with the absurdity of people, who could in principle kneel side by side to share the communion of Christ's body and blood, also planning revengeful slaughter against each other.

Mediaeval Christians seem very odd to most of us today, and nothing is helped by romanticizing them in a G.K. Chesterton style. But there are points at which they really do challenge us very sharply. They had a certain instinctive sense that symbols were not a matter simply of decoration, but both declared and actualized certain policies for meaningful living. Thus there were, for them, situations in which they could not treat actions as 'just' symbolic. When King Henry II refused to give the kiss of peace at Mass to Thomas Becket, he was a better theologian than he knew. He recognized that giving the kiss would not only suggest that he *was* at peace with Thomas (which he was not) but would also commit him to *seeking* peace (which he did not want to do). He knew well enough that he had no intention of giving the symbol room to work; and so, rightly and honestly, he sinned boldly and refused it.

Imagine for a moment a far from impossible situation: an East German Christian attending a parish communion service somewhere in Britain. Would anyone be so rude and unwelcoming as not to shake hands with him at the Peace? of course not. Very well; but what are we expressing and what are we seeking in such an act? How far do we in fact intend to 'give room' to this symbol?

I know that this is an unfair and strained analogy, and I use it only as a reminder that questions about international reconciliation are not always abstract and far away. Recently, Dr Peter Matheson of Edinburgh produced, for the Scottish Methodist Peace and Justice Centre, 'Ninety-five Theses' on nuclear warfare; the third of these very disturbing and sharply worded propositions was: 'Christ's Church does not cease at the Oder-Neisse Line'. He goes on to argue that, if the Church is a new humanity, a universal royal priesthood, its wavering commitment and uncertain voice on the nuclear issue is 'un-churching the Church' (thesis 32). How can a church that claims to be catholic – for all humanity – settle down with a situation in which its central symbols of reconciliation are put in question by the fact that those who celebrate them are divided by abiding suspicion, hostility, and planned aggression? If it does so, it is undermining its own deepest reality. For the Church is itself a symbol – of the 'catholic' love of God for his creation, the adaptability of his love to each and every creature; and so it is also a symbol of the truth that, because of the nature of this love, human beings have a common destiny. They are meant to be one, not in some super-personal collectivity or organism, but one in the patterns of their growth, the goals towards which they move. Each and every person, as the object of God's compassion and grace, has received a call to grow into free, conscious and responsible love. In this sense, there is *one* human future in God's purposes, and its unity is crystallized in the *one* story of a particular person, in his living and dying. That one life of full and mature compassion, acceptance and understanding is our future. Christ is the goal to which we move.

*

This is what the Church exists to say, and to sing, play, paint, act in all the ways it can: that human destiny, for all its unpredictable and irreducible differences, is in fact a single pattern organized around the magnetic centre of Jesus. And this means that my human vocation is part of the same harmonic whole as yours. To affirm my calling is to affirm yours in the same moment. If Jesus's humanity, Jesus's way of living and dying, is the shape of my future, so it is for all; no section, no class or nation within the human world, is excluded in advance from the hope of this calling. And thus there is not one Christian hope for one group, another for the rest – a point perhaps worth making against over-exclusive styles of black theology or women's theology or even liberation theology. In the long run, liberation is indivisible for those who truly believe that the world holds together in the one Word which is Jesus.

The Church, then, is a sign both of God's comprehensive, unified purpose and of its embodiment in Jesus; but also of the humanity that is to be – a global family, in which God's gifts are thankfully received *to be shared*, and all are involved in building up the liberty and maturity of all. The Church is a place where we are invited to look at one another with a kind of veneration, indeed, a kind of contemplation, delighting in the rich possibilities which our brothers and sisters have – and weeping over all those things which distort or block those possibilities. 'Who is weak, and I am not weak?' asked St Paul (2 Corinthians 11:29): the frustration or oppression of anyone is a diminution of my own strength and my own possibilities (which is why so many see certain attitudes to the ordained ministry of women in the Church as a weakening or a diminution of all ministry). So while the Church does not exist for the sake of peace, it is not easy to see how the Church can truly be itself in the absence of peace, in a situation where – by definition – people see the interests of various groups or nations as mutually exclusive.

But of course, because of the infinite possibilities of self-deceit in human beings, there will always be some such absence of peace. False and blasphemous goals are fixed, false models of humanity prevail. And in such circumstances there will be conflict, and rightly so – conflict sometimes between the Church and the society in which it lives, because that society is in bondage to idols. Indeed, much of the point of what I wrote in the first chapter was to suggest that we need to identify more clearly certain points of sharp collision or contradiction between the Christian vision and the prevailing mind of our society. In this sense, the Church is never going to be completely itself while history lasts – or, in more traditional theological terms, the Church and the world will never completely coincide. We live in hope, and to the extent we live in hope, we also live in creative dissatisfaction.

However, the Church does exist – not perfectly, but still quite concretely. Within its own life it is found to be a sacrament, an effective, compelling symbol, of a humanity able to live by sharing and by loving, reverent mutual attention. In its life it is committed to challenging the conventional conflicts of power and interest in the world. We all know how effectively a multi-racial Church can operate as a point of hope and criticism in a racially divided society. What we are less used to thinking about, perhaps, is the witness of a Church existing on both sides of an international conflict – especially an international conflict whose climax would be 'mutual assured destruction', if it ever broke out into open war. Here is a situation where one group of human beings announces, effectually, that in the long run its welfare and its survival will depend on the destruction of others. In these circumstances, the Church is bound, by its mere existence, to be a startling and challenging fact.

Cold war confrontation says that 'the others' are finally dispensable; they have nothing to give us that we could not do without. The existence of the Church contradicts this flatly, maintaining that we all need each other for our fulfilment, and that when mutual sharing breaks down this is a universal tragedy, a wound in the whole human race. The logical conclusion is indeed what a great Russian saint of this century said, that no one could truly know the joys of heaven so long as anyone remained in hell. And the same insight lies behind one of the central beliefs of certain Buddhists: no enlightened person, no 'Buddha', can enter into ultimate bliss while there are still unenlightened souls on earth. The greater the enlightenment, the greater the compassion; so the enlightened saint returns again and again to earth (like the Dalai Lama) for the sake of the ignorant and suffering.

If salvation is for any, it is for all. And Christianity in its way goes even further than Buddhism by coming near to suggesting that if it is not for all, it is not really for any.

The 'return' to the lost, the excluded, the failed or destroyed, is not an option for the saint, but the very heart of saintliness. And we might think not only of Jesus's parable of the shepherd, but of the great theological myth of the Descent into Hell, in which God's presence in the world in Jesus is seen as his journey into the furthest deserts of despair and alienation. It is the supreme image of his freedom, to go where he is denied and forgotten; he shows his inexhaustible mercy for all by identifying even with the lost. In some elusive and paradoxical way, this myth speaks yet again of one human destiny, realized in and through Jesus. He comes to his new and risen life, his universal kingship, by searching out *all* the forgotten and failed members of the human family. Only in this way can he claim 'all authority in heaven and on earth'; only in this way can his family be in principle co-extensive with the whole human family, past, present and to come.

Our hope and our faith as Christians is that Jesus is Lord – that there is no situation in which he is irrelevant or impotent. In all human experience, even the most hellish, he is present, his image can be found, as a point of creative protest, growth and change. And this we believe because he endured the extreme of lostness himself on his path to the throne of his Father; he enters into his glory in and through the enduring of our human hell. In other words, our faith absolutely depends on an unimaginable crossing of frontiers, the barriers between God and despairing, Godless men and women. It depends on the possibility of meeting Christ in any and every place, and in any and every person. The degree to which we fail to find him, see or hear him, in anyone, is the degree to which we have not grasped – or rather yielded to, been grasped by – his Lordship.

And that is why the Church is 'catholic' – for all, adapting itself endlessly to human culture and to human need, opening itself to all, and linking the cultures and needs, the various identities, the diverse roots, of men and women the world over. It strives to show and interpret and share the gifts of one person or group or nation, offering them to all; and to each it offers the resources of all. When it is not catholic, it is not truly itself (hence the seriousness of the division between Christian communions – the deeper the split, the less freely grace works in the divided groups, because they are refusing the unique gifts they should be receiving through each other). And when it is, however sporadically and unsurely, catholic, it is a sacrament of peace: not a peace of undramatic, tepid co-existence and noninterference, but a peace which is free, active involvement, compassion, grateful receiving, generous offering, reciprocal enrichment. This is the peace Jesus creates between God and world, because it is the kind of peace which exists between him and his Father. We shall be looking at this later in more detail; perhaps for now we can let it stand as a general and provisional definition at the most basic theological level of what the Church is about in relation to the life and death of Jesus.

*

So, returning to our starting-point: a catholic Church is one whose loyalty is to a vision of humanity as a single, though endlessly various, whole, a single pattern centred on Jesus. Its loyalties cannot be nationalistic or even ideological. Its very existence on both sides of an international ideological conflict challenges the all-importance or finality of that conflict. This does not mean that such conflicts are of no concern to Christians, or that Christianity is 'beyond' conflict. It *does* mean that any attitude which implies that the survival of my/our point of view/national security/purity of doctrine is so absolute a priority that no human price in the lives or welfare of others is too high to pay for it, is intolerable for the Christian.

Of course, people in positions of public responsibility constantly make judgements in which a price is paid in the welfare and the life of some: there is 'moral risk' involved here, and there is no point in minimizing its seriousness. Those concerned for peace too easily ignore its cost. Yet there is surely an irreconcilable collision; the Church really does relativize our loyalties, denying totally that the survival or success of one human sector or interest can ever be a final priority such as to justify the destruction of the dissidents. And when violence and destruction seem to be the only available options, in situations of deep and apparently insoluble frustration (the rule of a Hitler or an Amin), it is too cheap for Christians simply to condemn and to distance themselves from it. But it is impossible for Christians to rejoice over it, bless it or rationalize it. Insofar as violence always implies the dispensability of some person or group it is a tragedy which nothing can soften.

And so the catholic Church must be a standing challenge to all war-oriented policy; above all to a policy which deliberately and regularly speaks in terms of 'assured destruction', of retaliation and of a balance of terror. How could such rhetoric be justified, except on the assumption that our interests are a priority for which no price is too high – the very assumption which the catholic Gospel utterly contradicts? No Christian can use this kind of language without a profound betrayal of faith in the lordship of Jesus crucified, Jesus in hell, Jesus who fills heaven and earth with his compassionate identification, his breaking of barriers. The world is such that we cannot ignore questions of defence and security – only a moral imbecile could fail to see that; yet the concept of a *total* defence purchased by *total* threat, defence through the menace of mutual genocide, takes us beyond morality and reason as much as it takes us beyond faith and charity.

It undermines faith; and it equally undermines penitence. We saw in the first chapter how the social effects of planning for total war work against the possibility of responsible awareness and creative change by generating fantasies of impotence in the face of utterly irrational disaster. But here we are dealing with another kind of alibi for repentance. Repentance, for Christians, is intimately bound up with the hope of change – more particularly, of changed relationships. It is an acknowledgement of failure, based on trust in grace – which is the trust that no breakdown or severance of understanding and contact is ultimately disastrous. We are not forever 'frozen' in the attitudes of greed, envy, malice, manipulation and distrust which ruin so much of our lives. We are not fixed eternally in the distorted relation of oppressor and victim, rejecter and rejected. Repentance is our refusal to close our ears and hearts to the other, our confession that we cannot live without them. And although there are all sorts of situations in which we have no tangible guarantees that reconciliation with another person *is* achieved or realized, at least we have turned to them with our hands open. Our repentance, our turning around, has introduced something fresh, or rather, has recognized the possibility of grace, the hidden image of Jesus, which is already there in the situation, and allowed it room to emerge.

Planning wholesale destruction is planning impenitence. It represents a choice to fix or freeze relations in the state of total mutual rejection. When you have obliterated the other, in full consciousness of what you are doing, in order precisely to avoid any radical questioning of your own interest, your own secure identity, it is hard to see how penitence could be generated. Perhaps it could; but after a nuclear assault, it would (if it was going to be at all sincere) be massively traumatic and disorienting. There are those who have repented of their share in the Holocaust; far more seem to know that acknowledgement of what they have done would simply strain their sanity to breaking-point, and a merciful (though far from grace-ful) amnesia conquers (something I have tried to reflect on in an earlier piece of writing, on resurrection and forgiveness). And it is surely a question worth asking whether any society as a whole could sanely live with such a memory. Would not the result more probably be an intensification of just that desperate flight from responsibility we were looking at in the first chapter?

*

Planning for total war is a contradiction of catholicity, and a threat to the possibility of creative repentance. But somebody might well want to argue at this point that, despite all my woolly rhetoric about the awfulness of a 'balance of terror', I have ignored the fact that lives have been saved on a large scale by this admittedly depressing and disedifying balance. It is more than forty years since the outbreak of the last global war (at the time of writing . . .). The appalling scale of a possible third world war is exactly what has stopped it happening.

This is a serious argument. Once you grant (as I do) that certain kinds of defence policy and regard for security are inevitable in a divided world, should you not acknowledge that, in a world where any nuclear armaments exist, the only possible realistic defence, the only way of staving off slaughter on a huge scale, is to speak the same language as your probable enemies and guarantee that the price of any war is going to be impossibly high? It would be too much of a debating point, perhaps, to insist that calculations of a limited ('theatre') war with nuclear weaponry have made the whole argument a good deal more complicated, and the supposed guarantees rather less clear. What is of more concern in relation to the theme of this chapter is the sense in which mutual threat really has preserved peace.

Because the deep – and often unrecognized – irony is that it has done so by 'draining off' violent and bloody conflicts away from Europe and North America. Conflicts between the major powers are fought out in the Third World. Given that it is not safe to open an outright conflict with conventional arms in Europe because of the risk of escalation, the convenient solution is armed struggle with the forces, official or revolutionary, of a country or countries not supposed to possess a nuclear arsenal. In fact, since no one has yet succeeded in producing a watertight non-proliferation agreement, and pressure upon smaller nations to develop nuclear arms is stronger and stronger, this is an increasingly risky habit. But even if it were not so, it would remain a morally outrageous one. Our lives are being preserved at the cost of a constant stream of more expendable human resources, African, Asian, Latin American. Sometimes it is a question of open war, as regularly in the Middle East; more often of thinly-veiled involvement in a civil war (Vietnam, Angola, Ethiopia in its genocidal assaults on Eritrean separatists), or simply of the 'stabilizing' of a nation by supporting oppressive and sometimes monstrous governments, whose ideological foes are the same as those of one or other major power, even if their positive principles do not correspond all that well with those of their patrons.

Neither of the world's power blocs is in a particularly secure moral position over this. What it means is that in fact the pure 'balance of terror' has failed to create a real equilibrium; it needs to be supplemented and supported by countless minor demonstrations of 'seriousness of military intentions', conducted at second-hand. It must be established, it seems, that both sides are willing to shed blood – though not each other's. And so the nations of the Third World gradually become hostages, progressively mutilated by their captors to show the strength of the latter's bargaining position. So far from the nuclear balance saving anyone from paying the price of war, it ensures only that the price is not paid by the chief contestants.

Most Christians now agree in deploring the effects of colonialism at its most ruthless. Indeed, most Christians, however sensitive and conscientious, are probably tired of being harangued on the need for international economic justice, because they do believe it to be an imperative, but are unhappily aware that it will not come about very rapidly. I am sorry if this just increases the unhappy and beleaguered frustration of so many good and honest people: but I fear the point has to be made. If we are to be concerned about the economic injustice done to the poorer countries of the world, we must be equally concerned about the way they are used in the conflicts of the great powers. And we have to ask how far such military colonialism is actually implied in the 'balance of terror' situation, even required by it.

It is a point that brings us back yet again to the 'catholic' vision of humanity proclaimed by and in Christ's Church. The security of Europe, North America and the Soviet Union is not to be purchased by the lives of Vietnamese, Eritreans, Poles, Afghans, Turks, Salvadoreans or black South Africans, because the catholic Church affirms one humanity and one destiny for all. The frustration of some cannot be an organic element in the fulfilment of others. The potent and liberating utilitarian axiom, that action should be judged with reference to the greatest good of the greatest number, has in our time been perverted into a search for the greatest good of the greatest number *whatever the cost* to the few – not what the classical utilitarians meant. And Christian faith looks to a God whose purpose is the fulfilment, not of the majority, but of all. Jesus had harsh words for those who lock the door of the Kingdom to others, and do not enter themselves (Matthew 23:13); and much of his teaching implies the corollary that to shut the door to others *is* to shut out oneself.

This may seem an extreme reading to some; no one is 'denying the Kingdom of Heaven' to others. Consciously, no: but the implications of what we do must be faced. And a policy which, by calculating on mass destruction, on indiscriminate slaughter, treats large parts of the human race as dispensable necessarily assumes that their humanity is to be taken less seriously than ours. And if it preserves its equilibrium by trading off the lives of impotent third parties, it compounds the monstrosity. What I have tried to argue is that to take the humanity of others less seriously than one's own is to imply that their human vocation is less important than, and so different from, ours; and that that is to deny the vision of a single humanity summed up in the second Adam.

Let me say again that I *do* recognize that practically every society is driven to secure its stability by policies that are in some degree coercive, and to that extent do not treat all as, in all circumstances, having what Aquinas called 'equality of liberty'. In simple terms, all states have laws and prisons, and depend on certain sorts of institutionalized threats. But a society which secured its stability by indiscriminate terror, or by systematically victimizing a 'scapegoat' minority, we should rightly judge to be a tyranny. Sanctions against criminals we accept; we do not normally accept the Old Testament system of sanctions applied against criminals and all those innocently associated with them (see, for example, Joshua 7:24–25). This would now look like indiscriminate terror. Why is the moral colouring so different when applied to entire nations? And does not the fate of the poorer countries caught up in all this look rather like that of the impotent and despised group onto whom the aggressions of the majority are projected? – though in this case, of course, we are not dealing with a minority . . .

No; the argument from the peacekeeping effectiveness of the nuclear balance is not such a very clear and satisfactory one, certainly not so long as it refuses honestly to face the implications for the rest of the world. I do not think a Christian can avoid the issue in this way. We are still left with something that affronts the singleness of Christian hope, that undermines faith in Jesus as the form and face of a new, reconciled humanity. We are still refusing to *look* at certain other human beings in the trust that we shall see in them Christ's image. And it is that failure to look which cuts us off from certain specific human embodiments of grace, and so from the fullness of our own hope and salvation.

*

The failure to look, or, to revert to a word used earlier in this connection, the failure to contemplate. Contemplation is what is due to God; due to him because he is inexhaustibly what he is, resisting capture and analysis, always more, always further. But he has not left himself without witnesses, because the world is full of phenomena which, although they may be analysable on one level, resist any kind of total assimilation and continue to invite and question. Art at its best does this. In fact, anything which invites us to the pervasive awareness of a world beyond the power of the ego invites contemplation; which is also why contemplation is inseparable from delight and love, which arise in their full reality, life, and growth only when we are taken out of the sterile closed circle of ourselves and our plans, projects and expectations. 'It was not possible for man to know himself and the world, except first after some mode of knowledge, some art of discovery. The most perfect . . . art was pure love. The approach by love was the approach to fact; to love anything but fact was not love.' Thus Charles Williams, in his most successful treatment of the triumph of illusion and self-gratification in human relations, the novel *Descent Into Hell*. No love without contemplation, no contemplation without a mind and heart open to receive and not seeking to create its own world out of the nothingness of the ego and its fantasies.

Contemplation for men and women is looking and listening and being moulded by what is other. It is recognizing that you are created – limited, living in time – and allowing yourself to go on being created in and by the world of things and persons in time, all of them mediating the obscure universal initiative of an uncreated action, so wholly regardless of 'self' that it lets the whole universe be. Creation is there because of the limitless capacity of *God* for contemplation – allowing the other to be, and engaging with the other, shaping a common story of God and the world, a shared 'drama'. God allows himself to appear in the form of limitation, as if he needed us for his delight and fulfilment – Christ calling for his bride to come out to him and perfect his joy. It is on this that St John meditates in the 'Farewell Discourses' in his gospel.

God contemplates the world out of his own freedom; it is both his freedom and his nature that he acts to involve himself in covenant and in family relationship with us. It is because of the inexhaustibility of his love that he can show himself in and through limited and mortal beings, in creatures. But we, who are creatures by nature, begin with limited freedom and limited love; so that for us contemplation is something we have to choose and learn and grow into. For God, it is saying Yes to all creation; for us it is saying Yes to our *createdness*, and through that, saying Yes to the createdness of all other things. God in a sense does not 'need' to love and to contemplate a creation: he is in himself attentive love at its highest (which is part of what the doctrine of the Trinity affirms). He loves, speaks, communicates, delights and shares because it is his nature. But what for him is nature is for us destiny, vocation. We are in time, and thus what we are we must grow into. We *do* need contemplation, we need to learn selfless love, because for us there is always the possibility of failing to grow as we should. So we need to live in a world constantly inviting us to contemplation, a world which will not leave us alone, feeding only on ourselves – a world which delights us and which assaults us by its strangeness, its resistance to us. And, above all, a world of persons, in which we can be invited to love by finding ourselves the objects of love, where we learn contemplative attention as we are ourselves attended to.

I hope this will help to make it rather clearer why a system which denies or threatens the contemplative possibilities of human beings is a revolt against the creating will of God. We speak of a nuclear holocaust – perhaps almost too glibly – as 'apocalyptic', as the end of the world. And there are not lacking those who say there is a certain lack of faith in undue fear of the end of the world-as-we-know-it, since God's providence is always capable of working through and beyond disaster. True, of course. But it quite ignores the fact, laboured enough already in these pages, that war is not a natural disaster. It occurs because of human greed, fantasy and destructiveness – that is, because of sin. Sin is fundamentally a refusal to accept creatureliness, the struggle to remake the world around myself; it is a refusal of contemplation. To refuse contemplation is to refuse God's creation, and so to reject love. And if hell means anything, it means this. It is this we fear, and rightly fear. Not 'the end of the world' as a catastrophe at the material level (as if that were not bad enough), but the *unmaking* of the world, the system of created relationships designed for sacrificial love – a massive and ultimate revolt against the will of God. Let me reiterate what I wrote earlier: war is to be dreaded because it destroys both body and soul, because, in our present circumstances, it points to hell.

Professor Donald MacKinnon, in his 1981 Boutwood Lectures on 'Ethical Problems of Nuclear Warfare', spoke of the modern nuclear state as confronted by unprecedented temptation – the temptation to try for 'total victory', 'to yield to a fundamental impatience, the end either total victory or nothingness'. And this is most suggestively linked with Milton's presentation in *Paradise Regained* of the culminating temptation of Jesus by Satan, to cast himself from the pinnacle of the Temple. 'Milton saw Christ tempted impatiently to escape the burden of his human existence. We live in an age in which such a temptation is not far from every one of us; for we have to learn anew what it is to be human.'

What it is to be human: to be a creature, a part of the world, a moment in a pattern, dependent on others, others dependent on ourselves, called therefore to contemplation, without which there is no growth or fullness. Isolation is the refusal of humanity; and that includes the isolation of my or our needs from those of the human world. Beyond it stands the Luciferian impulse to destroy reality for my sake, the impatience with the weary burden of creatureliness. Creatureliness means, after all, never having 'done with' people or the world around or God. It means the risk of response, decision, listening and answering, *attending* to a constantly shifting environment. But to reject all this, hugging to oneself the diabolical knowledge that it could all be ended if we so chose, is the beginning of hell – like Marcus Aurelius' chilling remark that you may console yourself in misery with the reflection that you are always perfectly free to escape from life, though it might be improper actually to do so. That frigid irony has not a little to do with the psychology of nuclear deterrence. It might be improper to use our arsenal; but it is a consoling sign of our Godlike liberty that we could. Our liberty is thus seen as freedom to cut our ties, to unravel the knots binding us in one world, to break the humiliating cords of interdependence; liberty to be unreal, to commit moral – if not physical – suicide.

God's liberty is not so. His freedom is seen in the creation of bonds and networks of sharing, making a world which he wills, in Jesus and his Church, to be engaged. If we seek Godlike liberty, it can only be through the acceptance of that same world – with all the risk involved, the uncertainty. We must say No to the temptation to diabolic detachment, the privacy of Satan; and we must learn the patience of attentive love. Through that vulnerability true peace is made, in us and for us.

Yet, of course, it is an elusive thing. 'Peace' can be the ultimate consoling fantasy, and we need all our alertness to see that it does not become so. Before going on to explore something of what is positively involved in peace-making, we must have a critical look also at some of our illusory images of peace. To this we shall turn in the next chapter.

CHAPTER 3

ILLUSIONS OF PEACE

People go to stay in the guest-houses of monasteries and convents (in surprisingly large numbers) to absorb an atmosphere of 'peace': it is a break from conflict and tension, a move into another world from which strain is supposedly absent. The world of the cloister is one in which some new level of awareness has been attained, and its inhabitants breathe a different air. And we, less fortunate (or less committed), are briefly admitted into it, for our nourishment and refreshment.

We all, in fact, badly need images of achieved repose, of a state in which the process of 'becoming' is in effect over; and we are increasingly fascinated by the contrast between 'being' and 'doing', and more and more inclined to think that a great deal of our civilization has been badly wrong about the balance between the two, overstressing acting, making, imposing change. It is true, too, that a lot of the central images of Christianity are not reposeful: however much the cross of Jesus is softened and formalized, however much the naked figure is clothed as priest or king, it remains an image that speaks of incompleteness, of a world of unreconciled conflicts, because it is inescapably the image of a man being tortured to death. We need something for daily consumption that is a bit less 'unfinished', and so, understandably, we turn to images of the sacred that are more still, more rounded or balanced. Certainly the popularity of the image of Mary has something to do with this – the innocence of virginity and the 'finished achievement' of motherhood hauntingly combined in a symbol of purity which also manages, uniquely, to be a symbol of nurture and inclusion, not simply of remoteness.

And the holiness of the cloister can be a corporate symbol of peace achieved – a thought superbly expressed in Hopkins' little poem, 'Heaven-Haven: A nun takes the veil':

> And I have asked to be
> Where no storms come,
> Where the green swell is in the havens dumb,
> And out of the swing of the sea.

This means that Christians living a monastic life have laid upon them an enormous load of expectation. They are called (not by God but by the Church) to make their lives, individually and communally, images of 'peace'. And thus people often feel very deeply hurt and betrayed when such images are broken; when someone leaves a community, re-enters 'our' world, as if to say that there is no decisive release from struggle, that the wheel can still turn. The world of the cloister is not so 'finished' after all, not invulnerable to strain, frustration, unhappiness and the heavy responsibility of choice. Of course we go on as usual with our fictionalized cloisters, full of people with no history, no record of change: the second-rate novel or film blithely continues to present us with the calm, bland stereotype of monk or nun (especially the latter), dedicated but basically untormented. But the closer we are to the reality of the lives of those of our fellow Christians living the religious life, the emptier this fiction becomes, and the clearer it is that the consoling peacefulness we demand to see embodied in them is not there for the asking. We do a serious injustice to the cloister when we dictate its terms of reference to it. Nor is it any excuse that there is also a monastic rhetoric which goes along with the world's fantasies: however lovely and seductive this is (as in Hopkins' poem), it is essentially untruthful; and no one knew that better than Hopkins himself in his own religious life.

Those upset or dissatisfied by Christianity's reluctance to provide adequate images of repose and fulfilment will be liable to look elsewhere. Much of the attraction of Buddhism for the liberal Western mind surely lies in this area: here is a style of action and response (not exactly a 'faith') in which the focal picture is indeed one of repose and disengagement – 'peace' in the sense we desire. The Buddha in meditation, eyes turned inward, so to speak, appears to the Western observer as a symbol of the achieved state in which conflict disappears; it can even, in its simple solidity, look like a figure without tension or the need for balance. Some writers, Eastern and Western, have indeed compared this favourably with the tortured image of the cross, and have made the valid and searching point that the cross itself can become a tool for an unhealthy and destructive obsession with pain. Yet the outside observer of the Buddhist world is all too liable to forget that even this image of repose and transcendence of conflict belongs in a far wider context of story and symbolism and ethical doctrine: balance, flexible imagination ('skill in means'), even conflict all have their role in the Buddhist spectrum. The Buddha's repose is indeed a state 'outside history'. But it represents a balance continually sought and renewed in historical life, and one which (at least for a very large section of the Buddhist world) is expressed in active compassion, a voluntary return into the world of suffering for the sake of those still imprisoned and unenlightened. The ultimate rest of *nirvana* is an idea, a myth, constantly interacting with the dynamic structures of worldly life, not a state of peacefulness objectively existing 'somewhere' and possessed by some individuals.

I have brought in the case of Buddhism because I believe that a lot of Western misreadings of it show very clearly what sort of illusions of peace we often work with. It is true that Buddhism's absolute is something defined wholly in terms of negation and absence, a state of utter motionless emptiness. But our temptation is to confuse this austere conception with the kind of 'rest' we normally experience. I act busily and tiringly, then stop for a period, and consciously enjoy my rest. This is a state in which I do not have to choose or act, in which obligations and responsibilities are lifted from my overburdened shoulders; and it is most appealing to think of such a state continuing indefinitely. The timeless calm, the serene half-smile, of the meditating Buddha look to us very like such a state prolonged and made habitual.

But *nirvana* is not to be enjoyed: because it is the end of the busy, greedy self and the curious and ingenious mind, there is no one there to enjoy it. It is real and final death (and nothing could show more plainly how little we are prepared to face death than the indulgent language of rest and sleep we so often use about it); and so it cannot satisfy our unhappy longing for a comfortable repose. I believe that, in fact, the *nirvana* idea has a lot to say about authentic peace, but we shall come back to that later. The point here is that the peace we are often interested in is essentially a state of passivity: peace means *not acting*, not having to choose or involve myself. And this links up with what we examined in the first chapter, the eagerness so many people feel to shed responsibility.

Those who criticize peace movements and disarmament campaigns often make the charge that the pacifist, or 'nuclear pacifist', is actually seeking to deny responsibility in just this way. The search for peace is a search for purity and security without any readiness to accept that there might be a price – even a moral price – to pay for security; it is a passion to keep one's hands clean, to avoid the possibility of guilt and the hard and inevitably compromising choices of practical politics. Now I believe that this is a gross and dangerously perverse interpretation of the deepest motives of the peace movements; I have tried to indicate already how I believe the real irresponsibility, the real obsession with purity and security, and the real refusal of guilt lies with those caught up in the 'war game'. But for all that, this is a serious criticism and not completely irrelevant to some kinds of talk about peace.

When, in the late sixties and early seventies, 'peace' became so much a catchword and a slogan among European and (even more) American youth movements, it came as part of a package which included a deep suspicion of public life and social planning, an idealization of small, intensely interrelating groups, and what might best be summed up as a disbelief in original sin – a conviction that humanity could be drastically reconstructed by good will or love, a certain denial of history and guilt. 'Give Peace a Chance' was the cry of a sub-culture apparently persuaded that peace was a natural state of organic harmony between human beings which would 'happen' when once the obstacles of hostility and suspicion had been overcome. There is more than a hint here of the idea that peace is what is left when social constraint and its resultant tensions and self-doubts have all vanished – so that peace appears in rather negative terms. Unjustly so: there is also some sense of peace as a mutually enriching harmony. But overall it is difficult to deny that this represented a limited and in many ways naïve understanding of peace, even a sentimental one. It was a view which opposed peace to history. Peace was seen rather as a sinking back to *natural* harmony, an escape from the over-complex world of large-scale political decisions and from the obligations of assessing the effects of personal history (what sort of capacities and limitations have been formed in me by my past experience?) and social development (how am I involved in the wider structures of society?).

Against this sort of attitude, the accusations of disengagement and irresponsibility have some real weight. Peace seen as escape or release is not an ideal easily communicated to those who are bitterly aware of their involvement, like it or not, in a world of interrelations. In our present context, as we have already seen, there is a longing for the sense of innocence; and if one aspect of this is (as suggested in the first chapter) an eagerness to disclaim responsibility for the public violence of international politics, another is certainly the rhetoric of peace as a 'natural' state of human relations, which is there for us to slip into once we relinquish superficial feelings of aggression and memories of the violent past.

The cause of peace is not much served, I believe, by insisting that violence is an unnatural aberration. It isn't necessary, of course, to run to the opposite extreme of emphasizing the innate aggressiveness of human beings in such a way as to rationalize violence as an entirely natural thing, quite beyond moral criticism. But we do live in an extremely delicate situation, looking for an elusive balance: we are receivers and dependants in all sorts of ways, we have no choice but to be receptive towards the world and others; yet our distinctive humanness depends on responding and modifying what is given us – asserting a unique point of view, a self, that needs to give and express itself and define its place in the world. It is really a rather silly question to ask whether we are 'basically' passive or aggressive: the truth is that we all experience ourselves as both receivers and givers. We 'open' our-

selves to the world and others, but we also need
self-definition, boundaries. We have to discover our
particular place, our identity, in interaction with others –
which always involves a refusal to be swallowed up by
others, and so therefore a degree of self-assertion, even
aggression. Without this we impoverish both ourselves
and the human world – remember what was said in the last
chapter about the need for all possible 'images of Christ'
in humanity to be uncovered and realized.

But such is the variety and – increasingly – the
uncontrollable rate of developing impressions and stimuli
that it is easy to feel it not as nourishment but as assault;
and here assertion slips into violence – the 'defensive'
pre-emptive strike: attack before I am attacked; make sure
I do not lose control. And the elusive balance is that
between patient receptivity and responsible, creative
acting. Discussions about the naturalness or unnatural-
ness of violence simply ignore the intricacy, the delicacy,
of the individual's growing processes in a human group.

*

So there is a model of peace which is regressive, a longing
for what is really an infantile condition: nothing happens
and there is nothing to do. There are never any decisions
to make, because the world is not perceived as a place
where clashes of principles or desires or goals occur. This
is indeed another variety of the social diseases we have
already looked at: and it is not surprising that, throughout
the history of our civilization (and of others too), periods
of social and political degeneracy have seen the rise of
movements that can be called regressive in this sense –
washing their hands of memories and compromises to
recreate a state of nature, turning their backs on history
and politics.

And also, very significantly, turning their backs on

language. The way we use language is a very clear sign of how we are all givers and receivers. We are born into it, yet it is an inheritance that means nothing – literally – until we react to what is given and begin to experiment with it. If we simply reproduce what is given, the result is not really language in its full sense: parrots 'talk'; but it would be odd to say that they *use language* or that we converse with them. And we measure children's growth in intelligence not by accuracy in repetition, despite the impression given by most of our present examination systems, but by skill in producing what are for them new combinations of words and ideas.

Now the decline of language into formalism, inarticulacy or incomprehensibility must be seen in this connection as part of the flight from history and responsibility. When, in the language of the 'alternative society' groups of the sixties and seventies, we find an increasing looseness of expression, repetitiousness, reliance on formulas and passive unwillingness to argue, we are witnessing human speech in decay. There is a withdrawal from the risks of dialogue, of developing thoughts and images in contact with the speech of other people – part of the whole process of withdrawing from decisions and boundary-making, and so part of the refusal to be a self, an active participant in a group, giving as well as receiving. The way the very word 'peace' came to be used in some circles is a painful illustration of this. I have mentioned the song, *Give Peace a Chance*: no one could doubt its passion and its sincerity; but its deliberate interminable repetition intensified the suspicion of many that 'peace' was bound up with mindless, would-be innocence. Unintelligent passion and sincerity is not a very reliable tool in persuasion or transformation.

The trouble with a retreat from dialogue into the impregnable castle of cliché and repetition is that it encourages just the same process in those who might have been partners in dialogue. Idle and shapeless talk about peace helps indirectly in the creation of a language of war which is equally beyond criticism or discussion, and becomes a distinctive dialect of the impenetrable bureaucratic nonsense so characteristic of our century. Thomas Merton, in a brilliant essay on 'War and the Crisis of Language' (reprinted in *On Peace*, Mowbrays, 1976), demonstrates how the sinister and unreal jargon of war reflects the same hankering after 'final solutions' that underlies the whole mentality of the arms race. He quotes (p.142) the remark of a U.S. major in Vietnam in 1968, who said of a military operation: 'It became necessary to destroy the town in order to save it.' Merton comments: 'The symbol of this perfect finality is the circle. An argument turns upon itself, and the beginning and end get lost: it just goes round and round its own circumference.' The terms of an operation, the goals of a military effort, are defined entirely by one limited group: into their rigid speech categories are fitted the needs and responses of all other parties involved. Thus there can never be any need for justification, and there is no possibility of assimilating criticism. Two dreamers wander past each other in the night, one murmuring 'Peace, peace', the other mechanically repeating 'neutral' official records of atrocity: two comfortably self-sufficient and final languages.

Merton makes some sharp and telling points about the sudden burst of charismatic phenomena in the American South at the time of the early civil rights demonstrations, the Cuba crisis and the beginnings of American involvement in Vietnam: 'At a time when the churches were at last becoming uneasily aware of a grave responsibility to *say something* about civil rights and nuclear war, the ones who could be least expected to be articulate on such subjects (and who often had solid dogmatic prejudices that foreclosed all discussion) began to cry out in unknown tongues... One thing is quite evident about this phenomenon. He who speaks in an unknown tongue can safely speak without fear of contradiction. His utterance ... forecloses all dialogue' (p.140). It would be foolish to make this the basis of an accusation of irresponsibility against the modern charismatic movement in its entirety, of course: Merton is dealing only with a particular manifestation. But he does implicitly raise the question of how far some sorts of charismatic speech and behaviour can be signs of withdrawal and regression in a context of acute conflict. This is another setting, in fact, in which the word 'peace' itself plays an important and rather ambiguous role, and in which there can be a reduction of language to formulae expecting stock responses (this is undeniably the job of certain sorts of chorus). It is simply one more example of retreat and regression. And – as all serious charismatic theologians would be the first to recognize – it has little to do with the more challenging and more biblical idea of the Spirit of God being given to equip the believer for trial, and indeed 'warfare'.

The flight from dialogue into self-justifying, self-perpetuating jargon is, then, an aspect, and a very significant one, of a flight from adulthood, relationship, decision and creativity. To speak to another is to commit yourself, and to that extent define and limit yourself; but only in that kind of decision is creation, innovation, and thus human enrichment possible. There is a miserable link between militarized politics, consumer society, the corruption and decline of the arts and the cheapening and trivializing of language – in politics, journalism, advertising and worship. Fear of responsibility leads to the fantasies of popular fiction we explored in the first chapter, to the fantasies of destructive final solutions and the ultimate tidiness of suicide discussed in the second chapter; and to the regressive desire for a life without conflict and dialogue, the peace of the womb. Our inbuilt fears and our bewilderment in the face of a more and more complicated world make possible a pattern of political and international relations which pretends to meet these fears and puzzlements, but in fact collides with them and deepens them. This is the vicious circle of the 'developed' world today.

*

When dialogue decays, so does language. And when language decays, possible views of the world disappear. Language becomes a commodity passively received, manufactured elsewhere, so that the view of the manufacturer prevails. '*Most* people do not or will not think round and beyond the language they consume, or maybe have not acquired the skill to do so. So they use whatever words and phrases they are given. The words and grammar of a language can codify a view of the world (including a view of nuclear arms), and . . . the language itself confirms, reinforces or even directs people's attitudes and beliefs' (Paul Chilton, in the CND magazine *Sanity* for October–November, 1981). And to criticize and protest against a manufactured, official language which mutes the realities of pain, death and social collapse involved in modern full-scale war, we need a language that is itself alive and alert, self-critical, capable of argument, exchange, and, above all, imagination – not a bland and self-indulgent counter-jargon. The task of the critic is to prevent a shrinking of possible views of the world, to resist any tendency to fix the limits of what can be thought. And so any healthy peace movement will be vigorously productive of songs and stories: it will communicate a sense of alertness to the oddities and diversities of the world – part of the dimension of contemplative delight touched on in the last chapter. Above all, it will not suggest a picture of peace as withdrawal, mindlessness or empty leisure. Nor will it pretend that reconciliation is something which will simply 'occur' when various obstacles have been removed.

For 'reconciliation' too is a seductive word. Probably most of us (certainly the clergy) have prayed for reconciliation at times of industrial conflict in this country. A pay dispute, a strike, a short-lived settlement – 'reconciliation' in these terms is almost bound to look like unhappy and unenthusiastic compromise. The professionals in this area understandably talk about 'conciliation' only: a much more modest word, suggesting, accurately enough, that the job to be done is really one of placating anger and pride, toning hostility down to a pitch of mere sullenness. Conciliation is only an episode in a continuing battle. To speak of reconciliation, as we use the word in talking of personal relations, or even of our relations with God, normally suggests authentically fresh possibilities, new beginnings, not a temporary cease-fire in a situation that remains basically unchanged. To use 'reconciliation' in connection with our public and industrial life is really rather strange, so long as we do not in fact expect or work for a change of structures, and think only of a readjustment, an overcoming of disturbances.

There is an illuminating analogy (suggested to me by a friend in discussion of the problems of industrial society) in the way we often think of health as the absence of sickness, and healing simply as the restoration and maintenance of a *status quo*. Such a picture is not false but, standing alone, it *is* misleading. It is just as important to conceive of healing as a process continuing throughout life, moving towards wholeness, and so of health as this process working in and through the 'conflicts' of disease or malfunction. It is a lesson we are slowly learning where medicine is concerned: 'healing' means more than the expulsion of disturbing symptoms by external force, but is also a co-operative with an organism trying to find and constantly re-create an equilibrium in its functioning and responses. 'Healing' may thus involve new departures in the life of an organism, and it will always facilitate adaptability. There is no static ideal state to which things must be returned.

Certainly, both reconciliation and healing in the Christian context have been seen as involving innovation, not only renovation. When St Ignatius of Antioch in a famous phrase referred to the Eucharist as the 'medicine of immortality', he obviously saw its healing power as a transforming one. And in the death of Jesus the reconciliation achieved between God and the world is pre-eminently a transformation, an expansion of horizons. We saw in the last chapter how Christian commitment absolutely refuses any 'freezing' of relationships, how penitence implies active change. Reconciliation, then, cannot be identified with conciliation and – in spite of frequent distortion – is not, for a Christian, a fundamentally conservative idea. If we pray for reconciliation in politics or industry we are – if we are theologically serious – praying for change and newness of life; not only changes of heart, but changes in the structure, the dramatic script, the concrete possibilities in relations.

Peace, health, reconciliation: all of them are images we are perennially tempted to see in passive, naturalistic, or static ways. All of them, in fact, can represent refusals of the world (even health, when fear of risking the stable mechanisms of a healthy organism cripples and immobilizes people); and when they are so, they subvert themselves. Because they are exclusive, limited states, defensive positions, they are always menaced from outside, by the flux going on around them, always being pressurized towards history – choice, commitment, movement. Thus they can be states subject to deeply ingrained anxiety which can be coped with only by more and more tactics of exclusion and withdrawal. And this in turn means a deeper isolation, being cut off from the world's flow of life: peace and health conceived like this eventually mean *death*, which is after all the ultimately stable condition. Yet, as we observed earlier, death is not to be sentimentalized into a long and comforting sleep, into womb-like cosiness; it is an ending and a void. Not, for the Christian, a hopeless void, but none the less the final blow to the self searching for security and gratification.

The search for peace and consolation for myself by increasing withdrawal and passivity in face of the world ends in the nonsensical situation of a self which only exists in the first place because it is part of a network of relations trying to survive in unrelatedness, which is impossible. I may try to buy peace at the cost of the world, speech, decision, action; but I shall find at the end of the day that I cannot hand over the world without handing over myself as well. I shall not be left to enjoy my sleep.

If we begin to understand this, the impossibility of peace existing in a human vacuum, we may see too the falsity or at least inadequacy of our projection onto certain men and women of an ideal of calm disengagement, peace without real and continuing cost. The popular concept of the peace of the cloister, like the glib misunderstandings of the Buddha's contemplation, is a damaging error – damaging to people who hold it, damaging to those onto whom it is projected. It encourages most of us to think of peace as something intrinsically separate from the hard and familiar world, something we cannot expect to see realized in most of the reality we know: and it demands the impossible from the cloister, increasing tenfold the real and heavy pressures of that life.

So, where politics and international relations are concerned, this idea of peace is one very congenial to those whose business is the war industry, and those whose interest lies in perpetuating the 'frozen' confrontations of conventional politics. 'Peace' becomes a beautiful, compelling and quite irrelevant thing, a counter to be moved around in the game, to describe an ideal situation which – fortunately – has no chance of coming into being. Those who insist on it as a present imperative can safely be dismissed as naïve, or else relegated to the category of those who have attained personal fulfilment (good luck to them!) at the price of living in a cramped and unreal world. The only peace which can exist now is a balance of hostilities. Two static views, in fact – peace as a natural state of repose, peace as a carefully maintained balance of basically immutable interests; peace as passivity or peace as 'conciliation' and adjustment, with equality of capacity for violence the balance of terror; peace as the deadlock between two blocs of bargaining power. So long as our views of peace are passive and negative, the field is left to *Realpolitik*, the supposedly rational and implicitly deadly calculations of deterrence and mutual assured destruction.

We are driven back again to the conclusion of the last chapter: God's peace has something to do with an acceptance of God's world in its complexity. Peace as passive repose is as much a refusal of contemplative love as is the nightmare of mutual terrorism. This may sound harsh to those who, for good reason, desire release or rest. Peace is attractive to many just because it promises solace, the lifting of burdens – 'There the wicked cease from troubling, and there the weary are at rest' (Job 3:17). But here we can only revert to the point made earlier: this is not a peace to be experienced, but the end of all experiences because it is the end of the self. Desiring peace of this kind is desiring death. It may be understandable, but it fails to give real weight to the purposiveness of human desire, awakened by a call and a prompting from beyond itself.

If we are indeed made as 'desirous' beings, drawn forward into growing and exploring by longing and hope, isolation and immobility cannot be intelligible human goals. And if peace is a proper human goal, it must be a peace different from the 'peace' of death. When the early monks went into the desert, longing for a repose free from the tumult of passion, no doubt there was an element of 'death-wish' in their search. Yet the goal as they saw it was the repose of communion with God, in which what had been removed were the barriers to active, 'reasonable' love. Their rest, their *hesychia*, was a state of sharing in God's activity, and so could and should involve an unconditional charity to others – 'dying to your neighbour', in the rather odd phrase of one of the Fathers of the Desert. The 'death' to be encountered here is the giving up of self-assertion, hostile and excluding judgement: the spiritual energy wasted, poured away, in resentment and censoriousness must be retrieved and woven into the concentrated simplicity of God-like love, the restored image of God in the soul.

This remains in important respects a static picture; but it is by no means as negative as it has often been represented to be. And it has little to do with a state of passive or regressive disengagement, sinking back to undifferentiated unity. It acknowledges the fact that we have histories, that we have to move away from primal repose and absorption, out of the womb into a world of movement and variety, and that if unity and peace are to be re-established, they will be radically different in kind from the restfulness of pre-conscious life in the womb. The ideal of the cloister is not as simple and consoling as

it at first appears. Indeed, it may have something
unexpectedly challenging to say to those outside. If the
Pax which is the motto of the Benedictine family means
more than a spiritual pillow for the weary wordly head, it
may suggest a model for that peace which *can* be the object
of authentically and actively human desire.

In the first instance, the monk of the fourth century
imagined that he was going into his desert solitude for
battle; and Benedict in his Rule still speaks of the monk's
'military service'. There is in this a protest against the
peace of adjustment and accommodation, the 'quiet life'
of Christians embedded in society. The really damaging
disengagement is in those who are unwittingly in bondage
to self-serving 'passion', and are thus incapable of free
action and clear-sighted love of God or others (as opposed
to the 'passionate' attachment which simply seeks to feed
off God and others). The monk's separation from family
and social ties is aimed at an overcoming of a far deeper
and more serious separation, the isolation of egotism,
which is the true cushion against reality. It is a release not
from love and choice but from self-protection, an escape
from escapism.

Dom Hubert van Zeller of Downside Abbey tells the
delightful story of a North Welsh convent where the
garden gate had at some point in a chequered career been
reversed – so that the side facing inwards now read
'Private' in large letters. The cloister was being warned to
keep its distance from the privacy of the world. This
reversal is no bad symbol of the necessary revisions in our
understanding of peace. The 'world', the unregenerate,
uncritical life of most human societies, is the place of
private, isolated existence, fear of facing the cost of
decision and involvement – haunted by the fantasy of
'peace'. Because it is already in a state of relative
withdrawal, it finds it hard to imagine peace except as an

intensified withdrawal; having begun to shrink from tension and struggle, its ideal of bliss is the total removal of conflict and all that stimulates it.

In contrast, the cloister abandons privacy for a solitude which forces people to confront their fear and evasiveness and so equips them for involvement by a stripping-down of the will. The point of the ascetic struggle against 'passion' is the development of an *unencumbered* will, free to unite and to co-operate with God's will, having shed the impulses to self-protection and self-gratification which limit and distort its horizon. So it is a lifestyle which at one level *invites* conflict, the conflict of which the rest of society is afraid, in order to allow a more truthful and courageous humanity to emerge. And the peace of the cloister lies in and through this particular battle.

It is probably obvious by now that the 'cloister' I have been talking about is not simply identical with the monastic institution (though the religious life remains an indispensable sign in a healthy Church of the seriousness of baptismal commitment). For we are *all* enjoined at baptism to be Christ's soldiers, and to join battle with untruth and fear; we are all involved in a protesting withdrawal from a society in which real engagement and creative relation have become impossible – a society so concerned to protect its illusory and uneasy peace that it organizes for a war to end wars. And final security through total war (as we saw in the last chapter) is a fairly openly self-destructive project – a kind of admission that the peace being sought for is indeed death. Against this, the believer is invited to 'choose life', though at the cost of the usual cushions and consolations for the individual – and the collective. The Christian Church is bound to be a protesting body; it will rightly ask of its members a degree of 'monastic' disengagement, a sustained willingness to step back into critical distance. It will ask for solitude –

distance from the tight huddle of fear, where people cling together to feed each other's fantasies. It will ask for silence – distance from the decayed and corrupting language of self-justifying and self-perpetuating cliques. It will ask for contemplation – distance from the manipulations and distortions of a self incapable of opening up to others. And out of all this will flow community, speech and action, all that we normally think of as the opposites of solitude, silence and contemplation. It is a death embraced for the sake of life – not the world traded in for the security of the self, but the fearful self surrendered in order to rejoin the real world, the truth of God's creation.

All this is laid upon us at baptism. But it is not imposed from outside as an impersonal imperative. Baptism speaks of a new identity *given* us – the identity of a particular human person who redraws the boundaries of what it is to be human. The impulse and the resource for our new commitment to creative disengagement, death for the sake of life, lies in Jesus of Nazareth; and what we mean by speaking of 'Christ's peace' is what we shall be examining in the next chapter.

CHAPTER 4

NOT AS THE WORLD GIVES

When the Jesus of the fourth gospel proclaims to his disciples, 'Peace I leave with you; my peace I give to you, not as the world gives do I give to you' (John 14:27), the assurance most Christians tend to hear in these words is of a peace more secure and lasting than any the world can offer. But this is not precisely what is said: 'not as the world gives' suggests both that the peace in question is not of the same sort as anything we habitually call peace, and that the giving itself is of a new and different order. What is offered and the way it is offered are alike a challenge to the world's peace.

In all strands of the gospel tradition, Jesus is not a figure readily associated with peace in the sense of visible harmony. He provokes conflict and confrontation, and says truly enough that he brings not peace but a sword (Matthew 10:34), that he comes to kindle a fire on the earth (Luke 12:49). In response to him, men and women discover and decide the basic orientation of their thoughts and wants: they are *judged*, and thus they unearth in themselves all kinds of hidden divisions and disunities. It may be true to say that through Jesus the world can discover a fundamental unity, a community of destiny; but it would be a fatal reduction of the Gospel to say that Jesus's work is simply the revelation of universal brotherhood. As has so often been said, it is hard to understand why anyone purveying such a bland message should ever be crucified. To preach a *natural* unity between all human beings as something simply to be seen and acknowledged takes us back to the fantasies of a natural state of peace and passive 'interlocking' which we looked at in the previous chapter. Before human unity can mean anything, we need to see why it is not obvious – how situations have been created in which there is no community of interest and purpose between people. We need to grasp in penitence how we have co-operated in fragmenting a world called to unity. And this does not mean scraping away divisions and distinctions to find an equality 'under the skin', but committing ourselves *in* our diversity to the creation of new and mutually enriching patterns of interaction. If our historical actions have created a divided world, our historical actions, our choice and speech and imagination, must create a world of positive mutuality.

And this precipitates the new and grave division of which Jesus speaks so sombrely – the division between the penitent and the impenitent, between those who see the world's calling to community and those content with fragmentation. The tragic impasse is that those compelled by the vision of community are driven by this vision to rupture many of the forms of communal living they are already involved in, because the uncritical acceptance of these forms implies an acceptance of the corrupt and divisive wider structures of which they are a part – or simply because these forms cannot tolerate the presence within them of a wider vision. The New Testament is haunted by the breach with the synagogue; Paul in Romans struggles to see how this destructive and bitter schism can be a stage in the creation of a wider 'peace' in God's mercy. Jesus himself, in the passages already quoted, is poignantly aware of the threat to the treasured harmony of family life. To receive Christ's peace is to share Jesus's own position as a sign of contradiction, and to be drawn into a course of action that seems constantly

to be deepening rather than healing the gulfs of understanding in the human world.

Can we somehow ease this dilemma by appealing to
some gift of 'inner' peace which provides the resources for
dealing with the confrontations of the world outside? Is
Christ's peace not the peace, the authority and confidence,
which characterized Jesus as a person? Certainly it is true
that when we talk about Christ's peace we must mean
some kind of share in Jesus's life or experience; but insofar
as we can say anything with confidence about what kind
of a man Jesus was, there seems at first little to reassure
us. The gospels do not present us with a figure marked by
any evident serenity – rather with someone in important
respects scarred by his own divisive role and painfully
aware of the costliness of what he is doing. He has to bear
the knowledge that he will cause the destruction of the
peace of Jerusalem (Luke 19:41–44); worse still, his
calling of Judas turns out to be a call to catastrophe and
despair, to self-damnation (Mark 14:21). He cannot spare
men and women the effects of his presence; and he does
not hold back his tears.

So he is a sign of contradiction not least because he is
himself so vulnerable to the contradiction he provokes.
The crisis, the dividedness, seems to run through his own
person. Spiritually as well as materially, it seems that the
Son of Man has no place to lay his head, but that he must
carry in himself both the compulsion of his calling, the
unanswerable command to be the Father's Son in all
things and to force the Kingdom closer, and the cold
clarity of knowing that his presence as the Son and the
herald of the Kingdom is for some an occasion of sin and
self-destruction. Without his presence, some might have
lived and died in their innocence (John 15:22). He must
sustain the urgent and transfiguring vision of an ultimate
mercy at last made plain and the knowledge that he cannot

make it so plain that all will see it. His irony, his imagination, his anger, his despair, his many-layered and even anarchic wit, all of them stem from the struggle to make visible to all what is to him so visible that it needs no description and escapes all description; and when he cries out against the obstinate stupidity of his hearers, it is because he has exhausted the resources of language and picture to no avail in trying to communicate to people what lies in front of their noses. He is at once eloquent and inarticulate; and at last, confronted with the rational politics of Caiaphas, he falls silent. 'If I tell you, you will not believe; and if I ask you, you will not answer' (Luke 22:67–68).

This is not peace as we see it. Jesus is a man profoundly not at home with his world and his contemporaries, and so in our terms a singularly unpeaceful person. And his isolation is not somehow smoothed over by a warming private conviction that all is well: his faith is a weightier and a darker thing than that. There is no peace for him on earth, in the present order. His life is directed towards the coming Kingdom – which is an order of peace quite different from the 'quiet life' we may long for. Jesus's miracles are often seen as 'signs of the Kingdom', clues to the fact that it is at the door; and they are miracles of freeing from bondage, healing, feeding, and life-giving. They speak of a realm where the Father's will is done by the removal of what actively damages and limits human dignity. And the recurring image of the Kingdom's joy is the feast of the royal Messiah, the king's banquet thrown open to paupers, cripples, rogues and vagabonds.

There is peace at the banquet not because nothing is happening but because people are reconciled, accepted sufficiently to relate to each other in love, gift and enjoyment. They are at home with each other and their host; they are at peace and they are *making* peace. But the food at the messianic feast, the supply of nourishment which makes it possible, is the love and welcome of the host. And when we in the present crisis, the moving world of time, anticipate the feast, we do so by remembering just how that love took final shape for us. Our food is the crucifixion: a body broken.

Yes, the Eucharist is the visionary sacrament of peace, the foretaste of the peaceful Kingdom of the Messiah. But the price of our sitting down in harmony is the echoing discord of the crucifixion, the memory of the unpeaceful end of an unpeaceful life. Our peace is only authentic, it seems, when the world's peace has been broken, exposed as false; when the passive consensus favoured by Caiaphas has been so upset that it brings out its latent violence against whatever disturbs it. Jesus's peace can only happen when such a crisis has been provoked. His own uneasiness, unpeacefulness, is a kind of persistent questioning: just how much of the truth can the world bear without arming itself? Can the world, the orderly society of occupied Palestine, 'contain' the announcement of a final compassion which confuses all barriers of purity and probity? Can this society be a *catholic* society? The answer is that it cannot contain such a vision. Jesus is, as Bonhoeffer put it, 'edged out' to the cross; Jesus's followers are likewise squeezed out of their religious milieu into a new community without the familiar barriers. The Church is what is expelled by societies as they struggle with the challenge of God's peace.

No social order is equipped to 'contain' this challenge: all are doomed to their varying degrees of defensiveness and dividedness, and the Church will always in our history be precipitated out. Perhaps the test of a society's health from the Christian point of view is how well it can continue to live with and listen to (not just tolerate) such a critical presence. For the Church, like its Lord, proclaims God's peace best when least preoccupied with maintaining a bland consensus with society, when it is most ready to be uneasy and constructively suspicious (and that is why it itself needs sometimes to 'precipitate' its own protest groups, like the monastic movement, as we noted in the previous chapter). It gathers around the Eucharistic table to hold together the present realities of struggle and breakage, and the hope of the Kingdom where we shall seriously, affirmingly and joyfully look each other in the face, at peace in Jerusalem. And again: we gather to recognize the way in which the struggle runs *through* us; in penitence, we look at our own refusals to be catholic, we bring to the surface our own resistance to grace. What we think of as the redeemed soul or mind or spirit is what is precipitated, drop by drop, in these regularly renewed confrontations with the defensive worldliness in each of us.

*

The trouble with all this is that it seems to make the present a time full of tension, and to reserve all genuine peace for the future. We are doomed to be so preoccupied with false peace, the tearing up of false treaties, the breaking up of deceptive harmonies, that the Church can come to sound like a strained revolutionary cell, in which present fulfilment is shunned for the sake of a rather vaguely imagined future. Irony, suspicion and dis-ease – the frame of mind we associate with figures like Kierke-gaard – seem to bypass the joy and peace which Paul (Galatians 5:22) describes as the *present* fruit of the spirit. We have, of course, stressed that the Church exists to show in the form of its common life the final destiny of the human race; it gives a place and a value to all. But what about the mental and spiritual life of the individual? Is this doomed to a perpetual anxiety?

man too in the sense that he evidently suffered from the constraints of his mission and its consequences. Is it only a kind of evasive or sentimental religiosity that comes to speak of peace in relation to his person – 'My peace I give you'?

The New Testament writers are not as a rule given to religious clichés where the person of Jesus is concerned, and they do not forget the irreducible elements of conflict in the experience of Jesus. Later theology unashamedly pressed the paradox: Jesus was in constant possession of the vision of God, as fully as any human being could possess it, even at the moment when his soul experienced utter dereliction. He 'saw' God as he cried, 'My God, my God, why hast thou forsaken me?' In him, it appears, the two worlds could co-exist. The seriousness of tragedy, the loss of Judas and Jerusalem, the torment of failure are pervasive; the vision of the Kingdom and the authoritative gift of love are no less so. His conflict and pain do not eat into his authority or diminish his assurance; nor is there any suggestion that the joy of the Kingdom blinds him to its cost or prompts him to retreat from present need and sickness. The one experience sharpens, deepens, the other.

Often, in the context of talking about the relation between religious vision and the needs of the world, people will refer to the transfiguration story of Mark, chapter 9, instantly followed as it is by the episode of the healing of an epileptic boy. Commentators have sometimes remarked upon what seems the clinical detachment of Jesus in verse 21, where, confronted with the spectacle of the boy in the throes of a seizure, Jesus pauses to ask, 'How long has he had this?' But the whole tenor of the story is far from clinical: Jesus is disturbed by the implication that this is a planned testcase, a symptom of doubt and curiosity, and accordingly refuses to react by 'automatically' mobilizing healing power. The boy and his father must emerge in their individuality, and the boy's condition must be seen as more than a passing phenomenon demanding a magical cure. How long? What is it really like? Are you and your son really *there*, do you have a story, a mind? Do you believe? And when the full suicidal destructiveness of the boy's condition is clear, and the honest hopelessness of the father is out in the open at last, Jesus acts.

Fanciful psychological exegesis is a temptation to be resisted. But Mark's narrative, with its laboured emphasis on the complexity and gravity of the situation, its refusal of formulaic brevity, is surely working towards the point that transfiguration not only fails to take away sickness and fear, but provides no way of avoiding or minimizing or generalizing them. Dramatically speaking, this is a Jesus grimly fascinated, almost obsessed, by the detail of what he sees; needing to see closely and without any softening. Perhaps this *would* be fanciful psychologizing. Yet it is not fanciful to see Mark making a deliberate and sharply outlined model of the Kingdom's tension with the world, and Jesus's awareness of it.

(And since 6th August has become Hiroshima Day as well as the Feast of the Transfiguration, this hardly needs to be elaborated. Suicidal, diabolic sickness still waits at the bottom of the mountain, though now there are more bodies to look at.)

Jesus transfigured, Jesus fresh from the glory of the timeless Kingdom, stands still to watch a single small incident of pain, mental and physical. The transfiguring clarity of the mountain top is here as well, picking out each detail with a new light. At the centre, Jesus stands still, in both landscapes; with Moses and Elijah, and with the epileptic youth. Where he stands is, not a middle ground, but a space where worlds overlap. In his life and person, he defines what it is for glory and misery to come together and interpret one another. The Kingdom conquers, but not by abolishing the memory of the world of human failure and distress; only by taking it into its life.

Jesus does not achieve a theoretical solution to the problem of how Kingdom and failure, future and present, hope and memory can be reconciled. He simply lives in both, the vividness of each, moment by moment, feeding the vividness of the other. He does so, the gospels suggest, because his life is given up, moment by moment, to his Father. Every moment and every experience is to be absorbed with utter seriousness – not in bland passivity, but taken, seen, probed and responded to. This is the 'obedience' of Jesus (never a very good word to describe this attitude of alert attention); and it is possible – so various bits of the New Testament suggest, and the fourth gospel argues explicitly – because he *sees* the Father. In the texture of all experience, joy, pain, vision, humiliation, Jesus acknowledges a single shaping love, drawing his life together into a single act of response. The world – or rather all the worlds, of grief and of hope – can be sensed as given, the material given us out of which to make a whole and many-faceted offering, a gift in return.

Jesus sees the Father, sees directly and unwaveringly, even in terror and death. The gospels do not give us any evidence for how he might have learned or grown into this perception, and all we can see is its unconditional presence. This sense of steady vision was almost certainly one of the things which prompted the conclusion that the life of Jesus was from its beginnings 'owned' by God and transparent to him – the conclusion gradually refined into a doctrine of incarnation. And however we may theorize about the process by which Jesus might have learned trust of this radical kind, the fact of it remains, manifest alike in authority and in vulnerability.

Trust: the conviction not that all will be instantly and visibly well, but that all experience *can* (though not 'must') affirm rather than destroy; an anchorage, a firm point, a still pivot. And this we might indeed call peace – the fact of recognizing an affirmative and immovable centre. Part of the experience of trust is to feel yourself to be the object of faithfulness: someone or something is dependable – and, in personal terms, that means that an option in your favour has been made and sustained. This is the Gospel, the revelation of God's identification with the well-being of the human world; a Gospel which can be proclaimed only by someone utterly absorbed in God's Yes to his creatures, so close to that universal and fundamental affirmation that he can be spoken of as God's word, image, child, and so on: 'All the promises of God find their yes in him' (2 Corinthians 1:20).

So in this light it is no empty formula to speak of Christ's peace. He is 'at peace' with the Father because he is aware that no experience can sever his anchorage in this root of his existence. He allows his life to be defined by what the Father gives, by the manifold and even tragic texture of history; but this is not a shape imposed from outside, because it calls out free response at every step. Out of the central solidity of seeing the Father and knowing his will, Jesus turns the same receptive and self-forgetting attention to all that lies around him. He is set free by his bond with the Father to feel the variety of human experience without defence, the violence of hope as well as the violence of suffering. When self is immersed in the affirming will of the Father, it does not need its customary protections. The fundamental peace is not a state of *feeling* as we normally think of it, but a fact of union, constantly apprehended in fresh and surprising ways, constantly looking for new embodiment as new situations arise. In this particular situation, what does it mean, practically, to be at one with the Father?

Not, indeed, a 'middle ground'. The worlds of future and present, hope and hopelessness meet in a perspective wider than the world itself. Jesus is a new world – a new creation – where earth and heaven, even hell and heaven, meet. His Gospel is not a generalization about the state of things, it does not say, like one fatuous modern formula, that 'the universe is fundamentally benevolent'. The Gospel is that Jesus's God is King, that the source of all things and the meaning of all things is what Jesus called *Abba*; that his reign is at hand, that the manifestation of beauty and significance in the world is always possible and always close; and so, that we can live now under the Kingdom, in readiness and hope, alert for the vision of the Father, without abandoning the world or trivializing our history.

*

Christ's peace, then, is given us as we are drawn into his world, as we enter his 'space'. When we hear the 'good news of peace', we do not comfortably relax in the confidence that a particularly tricky problem has been solved. On the contrary, we are invited to *live* in the world of Jesus – which means bearing, as he did, the tensions of knowing the full force both of hope and of grief. We can recall here, perhaps, what was said in our first chapter about the importance of learning again how to mourn, how to face without panic and flight the colossal damage done in our world to the dignity of men and women. We are free to face it, not because of any reassurance that it does not matter, not even because of any reassurance that God will make everything all right sooner or later, but because we are aware of ourselves and the whole world as objects of an infinite compassion which calls us to the same compassion and sustains us as we try to embody it. And, having seen how decisively in Jesus this faith can reconstruct the patterns of human relations and the forms of corporate life, we enter on the project of compassion, trusting in its re-creative power.

If Jesus creates a new world, embracing two diverse worlds of human experience, one helpful image for what he is doing is that of translation or interpretation. He does not allow either world to settle down in its own conventions, but interrupts it with worlds from elsewhere. Into the world of easy hope he brings the memory of hell; into the world of self-indulgent despair he brings the affirmation of love. Each world is extended and, as we have seen, intensified by the other; and preaching the Gospel may often be to challenge the settled stability of one world of experience by opening it up to the other – as in the story of Jesus, 'We piped for you and you would not dance. We wept and wailed and you would not mourn' (Matthew 11:17). Jesus consistently refuses to be drawn into the comforting uniformities of unquestioned collective emotions. Once again, he refuses to *belong*, but creates a world for others to belong in. His homelessness creates our home, a place for us to live.

And we can live at peace, in the Father's will. Jesus is homeless just because it is the Father's will that shapes his future, his possibilities, and not any earthly system; it is because he is at one with the Father, living in his peace, that he has no home elsewhere. When we are homeless as he was, ready to bear the world's tensions and challenge the world's peace, we receive his peace and his Father's.

It is indeed not the world's peace and not given as the world's is given. The peace of consensus or of quietism is given or imparted by joining in an act of exclusion. Illusory and corrupt forms of peace rest on a decision to ignore or repress certain dimensions of experience. But

Jesus 'leaves' his peace to the apostles on the night before he suffers, before he enters into the depth of the experience of death and glory together; and when he returns as risen, marked with his crucifixion wounds, he greets the apostles with, 'Peace be with you' (John 20:19 and 21). And his greeting is at once followed by the sending of the Eleven, as Jesus has been sent by the Father, and the giving of the Holy Spirit – which we have already learned, in John chapters 14–16, to associate with the renewing of the Church's critical and challenging nature, with the manifestation of truth and judgement and the unmasking of ignorance, deceit and evasion. This is a peace which does not exclude, but searches out the heart of things to embrace the dread and guilt which draw people away from truth – the peace of honest forgiveness.

So peace is given to Jesus's followers in the Easter event, the crisis of passion and resurrection which is the ultimate collision between truth and falsehood, life and death; and thus the giving of it is interlocked with the giving of the Spirit of truth. The Church is a community constituted in the Spirit who constantly recreates in its life the critical transaction of the cross: 'the last, the dread affray' is, by the Spirit's action, being refought daily and hourly in the Church's life and the believer's life. And it is here, in this battle, that the love, joy and peace of life in the Spirit are being daily and hourly brought to birth.

They are brought to birth because, in the struggle, we learn to experience grief, rejection, failure, without the paralysing fear of ultimate worthlessness. Our anchorage is in the strange peace of the cross and the empty grave – and so in the Father who brings Jesus to the cross and lifts him from his grave. Our peace lies in the God who is silent before our cries and protests, and yet does not desert or cease to create and call. Paul rightly speaks of a peace that 'passes all understanding' (Philippians 4:7). It leaves us inarticulate and even confused (and I have found it hard to write about with any clarity), because it is so evidently not a matter of comfort, solutions, repose. It is a rootedness in the place of Christ, the world of Christ, a deep reception of the truth that we are loved and affirmed – quite simply what a recent writer on 'The Inner Dynamics of Religion and Morality' called 'basic trust'.*

*

All self-respecting liberal Christians in the 1960s and '70s learned to sing (on practically every imaginable occasion, it seemed at times . . .) Sydney Carter's fine carol, 'Lord of the Dance'. The image of the eternal Word as dancing through the process of creation and redemption is not, of course, completely strange to Christianity. The second-century gnostic book, the *Acts of John*, shows Jesus before his passion bidding the apostles dance around him in a ring; and from the same period comes Clement of Alexandria's description of the dance of the heavenly beings under the guidance of the Word. Other theologians use the same image, and it receives its loveliest expression in Dante's *Paradise*. More modestly – but still hauntingly – there is the mediaeval English carol:

> Tomorrow shall be my dancing day;
> I would my true love did so chance
> To see the legend of my play,
> To call my true love to my dance.
>   Sing O, my love, my love, my love,
>   This have I done for my true love.

* Donald Evans, *Struggle and Fulfilment*, Collins, London, 1980.

But there have been those too who pointed out that the image and indeed the title, 'Lord of the Dance', belonged more in another religious tradition. *Nataraja*, the King of the Dance, is a major title and manifestation of Shiva, the Hindu deity. Anyone at all familiar with Indian art will know those countless figures of the four-armed god, dancing within a wheel of fire, one foot trampling on the dwarf who represents godless ignorance.

I do not think that the Hindu resonances of this image are any reason for suspecting it; and I mention it here precisely because the dance of Shiva is above all an image speaking of trust and of peace in the midst of what seems a profoundly menacing and hurtful world. Shiva, notoriously, is the god who combines sharp contradictions in his person. He is the creator and the fount of blessings; in the Tamil literature of South India, he is spoken of as consumed with passionate love and longing for human beings and their salvation. And he is also the destructive principle; not an annihilator, but a power that dissolves all forms to remake them, only to dissolve them again. He is in a special sense the god of time and death: he dances in the cemeteries, on the burning-ground, covered in the ashes of the dead. He is that which *limits* all earthly things, yet also that which connects them to each other, makes all things live again in other forms. Not surprisingly, some contemporary physicists have found this image the best way of crystallizing their insights into the nature of energy, flowing, dissolving and reforming endlessly.*

All this is contained in the icon of Shiva's dance. One foot firmly on the dwarf's head, one swinging high and free; the upper right hand holding a tiny drum – the drum which, when struck, utters the primal sound that initiates

* See especially F. Capra, *The Tao of Physics*, Collins, London, 1975.

creation – the upper left hand with a flame burning on it; the lower left hand facing the onlooker, palm outspread in the traditional gesture of peace. The whirlpool of reality has a still centre, the terrible God of instability and ceaseless motion points us to stillness and greets us in peace.

'*Not as the world gives*.' It may seem odd to go to India for an image of Christ's peace; but there can be few other icons which so remarkably embody the fusion of trust and tension in the Gospel. If we turn back from Shiva Nataraja to the crucifix, perhaps we shall be able to see more clearly how this can be itself an image of peace: here too, one hand holds the word of meaning, one hand holds the fire which questions all words and images. The contradiction is poised around a single axis, which in this case is the unique face of a human being – more than a cosmic symbol. Peace in contradiction is more than a truth about the energy of the universe. In Jesus of Nazareth, it has come to be an abiding dimension of mature, integral human-ness. The still centre is given to us as we give ourselves to this symbol, the cross of Christ, the tree of life, looking neither for escape nor for resolution, but only for a union with the will of the Father.

The cross is the culmination of Jesus's living-out of peace, not just because it is a symbol of the absorbing of violence without resistance and counter-violence (though that is important enough), but because it represents the total triumph in his life of 'the Father's will' – the constraint upon him of the deepest truth, the reality out of which he comes and which is closer to him than breathing. For him, passing through the cross is the final peace-making. It establishes in the world of men and women the truth of an affirmation and acceptance beyond all our destructiveness, untruth and pain, telling us that we may have a 'Father' also – that we may be trustingly surrendered to the source of our life and the life of all things, and receive into our minds and hearts the stillness of Jesus's offering of himself, the peace of the cross. It will not take away inner or outer conflict; on the contrary it will force us into conflict, into battle for the sake of the truth we have been given.

The 'violence' of peace-seeking and peace-making, about which people sometimes talk rhetorically, can only be the tireless readiness to assail our own longings for un-Christlike peace, comfort and safety – and it has to be wary of the characteristic temptation to psychological violence against others, dealing with our powerlessness by forcing others into guilt. All true; but the cross adds that we are not to be afraid, when the time is ripe for witness that *will* polarize, force an attitude into the open. And this can be experienced as a kind of violence by those under pressure from it. India, the U.S.A., southern Africa have all witnessed disproportionate fury and hurt generated by nonviolent protest, not only an intensified conflict, but an increase in actual violent activity and feeling by some. Part of what this chapter is about is the need to *feel* the tragedy of this without retreating into a castle of moral superiority; we have to recognize that conflict means that change is beginning. Whether for better or worse depends (not absolutely, but to a significant degree, perhaps) on our willingness to stay and bear the cost. And to do that requires the anchorage of the cross: trust, rootedness, faith and faithfulness. How this is formed and deepened in the lifestyle of the Christian we shall see in the next chapter.

CHAPTER 5

THE COST OF SIMPLICITY

Jesus's 'Blessed are the pure in heart' is – like all the beatitudes – all too easy to moralize. 'Purity', after all, has come to mean, in Christian usage, little more than a state of sexual innocence (certain delinquencies being described as 'sins against purity'), and 'purity of heart' will accordingly be taken as freedom from 'impure thoughts'. But for the Jews, the pure heart was above all the heart devoted to God without reserve, the heart of the person equipped to 'see God', to appear in his Temple, because of his or her integrity and single-mindedness, unswerving faithfulness. 'Who shall ascend the hill of the Lord? And who shall stand in his holy place? He who has clean hands and a pure heart, who does not lift up his soul to what is false, and does not swear deceitfully' (Psalm 24:3–4).

The pure in heart will see God: as the last chapter suggested, 'seeing the Father', the vision of a unifying love, drawing all experience together, is intimately related to directness and wholeness of response. Impurity of heart, which fails to see the Father, is the divided heart, incapable of giving itself without reserve. The impure heart qualifies its response with conditions, doubts, reservations, keeping its distance; it is incapable of that movement of supreme assent and desire which is love. Or again (thinking of the psalm quoted above): the impure heart is one prepared to settle for less than the truth, prepared to make do with the illusory peace of consensus and security. It is a heart which never wants anything enough to be intolerant of substitutes. Beneath its readiness to make do with less than reality is the fear of real desire. For real desire means the candid acknowledgement that I am incomplete and need something in order to be real myself. 'Impure' desire, on the other hand, assumes that *I* am solid and important: I take things to myself as my fancies suggest, as much as I want of this or that, so as to keep myself solid and steady. I *consume* things – to stop myself being consumed by real desire, which shows me my lack of solidity, my need to find and nourish my identity in and with others.

Real desire is about recognizing that I have no resting place: my home is what I must look for, eagerly, attentively, as I grow and journey. And – the Christian will add – my journey only 'ends' when it reaches God – and even then it does not come to a comfortable full stop because God is himself a region of unending new discovery and reappraisal and fresh vision. Pure desire is desire that longs to grow endlessly in knowledge of and rootedness in reality and truth. Impure desire desires to stop *having* to desire, to stop needing; it asks for a state where, finally, the ego can relax into self-sufficiency and does not have to go on stuffing bits and pieces of the world into itself in order to survive. Real desire can live with an unlimited horizon – which religious people call God – while unreal desire stumbles from moment to moment trying to gratify an immediate hunger, without accepting that 'hunger' is part of being human and so cannot be dealt with or understood by an endless succession of leak-plugging operations.

So the 'pure heart' relates also to the Mary and Martha story – Mary sees that *one thing* is necessary and directs her desire to that. It is not an allegory about action and contemplation, despite the long tradition of treating it thus, but a story about integrity and fragmentation – wanting one thing, and wanting all kinds of things. And thus it is also about how the self is understood, whether it is seen as being drawn into a magnetic centre, or seen as being the centre into which things are drawn. The question is, 'Does our desiring draw our life together, or does it break it up into a mass of passing gratifications?' Are we organized by some attracting force beyond our own selfhood, or does the self struggle to organize things around itself? In the latter case, we have in fact another manifestation of the urge for adjusting reality to *my* needs, the longing for peace on *my* conditions – a state in which movement and response and interaction will no longer be demanded of me. We have seen already how this is in itself a self-defeating effort, productive of fear and anxiety, and is, in the wider context, a death-directed longing – whereas the former option, our 'organization' by what is outside us, suggests a process of steady and abiding growth, 'eternal life'.

Jesus blesses the pure in heart as he blesses the poor, those who have the freedom to grieve, the unassertive (a pity 'meek' is so hopelessly negative a term in our ears), those who are passionate for the equitable community of God's Kingdom, the compassionate and the makers of peace, as well as the pure in heart; and it is difficult to think about any one of these without seeing how they all reflect on and make sense of each other. Purity of heart involves and includes poverty, the poverty of wanting one thing and not being distracted by many. Poverty thus becomes a freedom from anxiety and the desperate effort to shore up the precarious ego with superficial gratifications. And in this sense too, poverty is a lowering of defences; it exposes the self once again to grief, the possibilities of recognizing loss, frustration and tragedy in one's own life and the lives of others. So it makes mourning possible, and pity. To know mourning and pity makes domineering self-assertion unthinkable. Sensitivity to the depth and presence of others in their vulnerability rules out the bitter and harsh struggle for power in which others are made to pay the price of our fears and insecurities. Thus, inevitably, this involves the passion for equity, for a society where rivalry and struggle for dominance have no chance to grow; they grow on the soil of fear, of being threatened – and where, in the 'Kingdom', all are assured of the fact that they are loved and valued by the King, they have no root to feed them. And so peace is made. The beatitudes of Jesus, it has often been said, are far less a set of moral injunctions than a sketch of God's world, of what the Kingdom might be like. Those who see God are called his children, inherit all things, these are the children of the Kingdom, and their lives are marked by poverty, integrity and compassion. Their fullest and best interpretation remains Jesus himself; what they spell out to us is the shape of life lived in the Kingdom, Christlike life. They suggest how we might be, as Jesus was, a sign, in the tortured and broken present, of the healing future – present citizens of the Kingdom.

*

Poverty begins the list. Nowhere else does Jesus suggest that material privation and misery is good in itself (he has hard words for those indifferent to the wretched of the earth), and we must assume that he is thinking back to the familiar Jewish image of Israel as 'the congregation of the poor' – those who devote themselves to obedience so deeply that they have no defence but God. The poverty to be learned is dedication and dependence: dedication to the will of God, dependence upon the steady and faithful love of God. To be poor requires faith: that is why the 'poverty' of the beatitudes can only fully appear as a response to the good news of accepting love.

But it is also a response to the revelation that this compassion belongs to the final order of things, to the mind of God, so that it involves a requirement. To be in tune with the truth of things means being in tune with compassion, and this is the supreme *need* for men and women. This is what the 'order of things' asks from us for the balance and maintaining of the world in its interdependence. As soon as poverty is abandoned, we become preoccupied with possession (and so with rivalry and mutual threat) – the world being drawn in towards the self. New vortices of power and attraction are set up, the balance of mutual gift vanishes.

To see poverty like this requires a total shift in our understanding of need. Generally, we think of need as something *we* have which demands satisfaction – needs to eat, sleep, be loved, be needed. This is all very well until we draw the conclusion that anything which demands satisfaction is a need, and thus an imperative. But if we can see the need in ourselves as part of the balance of some universal need, we are less likely to mistake the momentary want for the true need.

This is a theme which both art and religion have considered in depth for literally thousands of years. Deeply rooted in all Oriental philosophies, from early Hinduism to Mao's Marxism, is the vision of just order: *dharma* in Hindu and Buddhist thought, *tao* in China. It cannot be described in the abstract, only sensed and discovered in the interlocking web of life as it is lived. It has often been a static, even an oppressive idea, especially when allied to the caste systems of India; but modern interpreters of the traditions have seen the error of associating it with any given order of society here and now, and have recovered much of its prophetic, critical and creative potential. It is a social ideal, but more than that alone: it takes seriously the relation of social and spiritual, and speaks of the necessity for an inner assent to the mystery on which all created harmonies rest (*dharma* comes originally from the verb meaning 'to support' or 'uphold').

And when the Jews of the post-exilic period speculated (as in Proverbs, Job or the apocryphal Wisdom of Solomon) about an everlasting Wisdom side by side with God in the process of creation, representing right order and right relation, they were expressing a similar concern. Even more strikingly there were already those in Jesus's time who believed that the Law, the Torah, had existed before creation: the rules governing human interrelation were not simply invented as a convenience but express the mind of God. It is with this in mind that Paul can use of Jesus the language that some of his colleagues would have used of the Law. Jesus is the image, the expression of God's mind: in him the wisdom underlying all things has utter freedom to act, in all he says and does.

So it was a sound instinct which led Chinese Christians to translate the opening of John's gospel, 'In the beginning was the *tao*', and to speak of the *tao* made flesh. In Jesus, the 'need' of things is made apparent: obliquely but unmistakably, the life and death of Jesus uncovers a pattern of sound relationships. He is a man who sees and answers this 'need', and so communicates its character and requirements to us; and in his resurrection, he returns to establish a community attentive to the need of things as manifest in him – attentive to *tao, dharma*, Torah, Sophia, and himself as the speaking embodiment of it. He is a poor man, never seeking to lure the world into the nets of his ego, but drawn by the wisdom that fills him towards the source of all, and drawing the world after him. Poor too in his defencelessness, his open-eyed exposure to mortal risk, because defence or retaliation would be a refusal of the need.

'Poverty' is the acceptance of being part of an interdependent order – being 'de-centred', in the language of another discipline. And thus poverty accepted and made one's own is, in practice, the testing and querying of supposed need in the context of a wider vision. Shakespeare's King Lear, challenged by his daughter to explain why he 'needs' a retinue of knightly attendants, burst out: 'O reason not the need! The basest beggars are in the poorest thing superfluous.' At this point in the play, menaced and desperate, Lear can only defend himself by a confused appeal to the 'need' for something over and above mere material sufficiency, and he seizes on clothing as an example. But later, faced with the isolated nakedness, material and mental, of 'Poor Tom', he collapses into madness: what he has to learn, on the 'wheel of fire' of his terrible humiliations, is the sense of a 'pattern of sound relations', justice and love. They are not to be explained in utilitarian terms – indeed, they survive very poorly on this basis. But they are the real answer to Lear's anguished question about the 'need' for more than is physically necessary. What makes human life significant, more than animal? Not clothing, not the acquisition of coverings for the naked ego, but the conscious participation in an order of compassion – an order revealed only as Lear experiences Cordelia's free mercy and pity – and mutual gift. Lear is right to protest at Regan's brutal utilitarianism; but he only knows how to answer her charge when he has been forcibly driven into the depth of privation, when his angry, terrified, grasping selfhood has been shattered by rejection and insanity – a dramatic instance of harsh polarization as a preliminary to healing. His forced external poverty drives him to the loving 'poverty' of compassion and penitence. He has learned to die, because he has learned to be part of a created world resting on will and wisdom.

The image of a cosmic 'need' is one that I have drawn from a recent novel by Doris Lessing. In the last three years, she has produced a sequence of brilliant and compelling works under the general title of *Canopus in Argos* – 'science fiction' stories, in one obvious sense, but in fact searching explorations of the levels of the mind. 'Canopus' is a planet in an advanced stage of cultural, mental and spiritual maturity, engaged in the nurture and education of a large number of dependent planets (including one disastrously unsuccessful and vulnerable planet known as 'Shikasta', 'the broken or hurt one,' whose history will be painfully familiar to all terrestrial readers). The hope of Canopus is to forge and maintain a link with its dependencies enabling them to reach the same level of consciousness. This is regularly frustrated by the hostile, violent and destructively greedy planet, Shammat, whose aim is a kind of slave empire; but progress is also held up by the machinations of a third power, Sirius – technologically sophisticated, inclined to despise or suspect the enigmatic Canopus, proud of its skills, but hopelessly at a loss when faced with the complex problems of long-term planning, and psychic-emotional adjustment which Canopus understands uniquely.

The second of these remarkable books, *The Sirian Experiments*,* focuses on the tension between Canopus and Sirius, especially in their dealings with Shikasta, where both are conducting evolutionary experiments. Ambien, the Sirian 'heroine' of the book, is shown gradually moving towards some grasp of the rationale of Canopean strategy – quite incomprehensible to the Sirian technocratic and bureaucratic planners. She interrogates Klorathy, the Canopean envoy, on the reason for the

* Jonathan Cape, London, 1981.

presence together on one colonized planet (not Shikasta) of two dramatically different species: is one meant to be instructing the other?

'No, I told you', he said gently. 'They are a balance for each other. Together they make a whole.'

'In relation to what?'

As I said this I realized I had come out with a real question: one that he had been waiting for me to ask. At once he replied: 'In relation to *need.*'

And my disappointment made me snap out: 'Need, need, need. You always say need. What need?'

He did not reply. (p. 195)

Later in the book, Ambien discovers a private note, jotted down by another Canopean official with whom she has been arguing.

How is it possible that an Empire (Sirius) can be so large, so strong, so long-lasting ... and yet never have any inkling at all of the basic fact? ... They let their populations rage out of control, and then suddenly limit them to practically nothing. And all this done according to a temporary balance of social forces and opinion – *never* according to Need. (p. 151)

The Sirians are unable to conceive of their function in relation to a whole, their place in a world, in an order; and so they are helpless in the face of questions of meaning, and essentially arbitrary, anxious and defensive, in their foreign and domestic policy. Their social life is uneven in its development and they are quite unable to avoid suspicious sectionalism; and their governing model in relations with other 'empires' is rivalry.

Sirius as a civilization is a myth of that level of awareness with which most of this book has been concerned. It is not openly and barbarously destructive, like Shammat, but its imbalances trap it in destructive patterns. And the basic imbalance is the development of technical and what could be called managerial skill in the absence of any parallel development of moral and spiritual sensitivity.

The result of such a disproportion is that there comes to be no way of evaluating technical development – so that it is instantly assumed that if a thing *can* be done it *must* be done. If a new technological refinement is seen to be theoretically possible, then it must be produced, regardless of cost, risk, or long-term consequences, and a market created. Of course all this is most obvious in the world of military technology. What fuels the arms race at least as much as national and international paranoia is the sheer energy and inventiveness of the armaments industry and its teams of researchers. Enormous profits are involved, so that there is heavy pressure on governments to invest in a spiral of technical development to which there is no obvious ceiling. President Eisenhower warned us, thirty years ago, about the growth of a 'military-industrial complex' which would effectively take over much of the decision-making from democratically elected governments: it was one of his most accurate forecasts. And (thinking back to the first chapter) it is alarming to think that the fatalism and impotence about the drift towards war felt by the average citizen is likely to be shared by governments.

But this is not the only area where 'need' is dramatically neglected, and development has been allowed to proceed uncriticized. Whatever the rights and wrongs of the growth of the nuclear energy industry, it is sadly undeniable that policy decisions have been made about its development in this and other countries which have bracketed or bypassed long-term questions about the social and economic effects of steady expansion (and now it appears that the major justification in terms of likely energy 'needs' in the future – i.e. maintaining present or higher levels of consumption – has been based on questionable calculations). Once again, the fact of spectacular technical advance has largely dictated choices: the question of appropriate alternative paths of research has barely been raised at administrative level.

Again, we have seen in the last few years some striking developments in information storage ('micro-chips', etc.). In terms of presentation to the commercial public, this has come over mostly as a package of fresh possibilities for broadcast entertainment: the 'video revolution'. This in itself is pretty ambivalent. The prospect of a culture in which people passively consume more and more quantities of bland popular entertainment, consoled by the illusion of having more choice because there are more buttons to press, is not an inspiring one. A free market in competitive broadcasting is not likely to produce that much material of a critical or provocative nature, if the American experience is anything to go by. And the assumption of most video entertainment technology is that entertainment is fundamentally a private matter: the individual will not have to move from his or her chair for anything. Activity or involvement is reduced to choice between the manufactured alternatives presented. No wonder it lends itself so well to the ultimate obsessive privacy and self-centredness of pornography.

But there is another side to this. New possibilities of information storage have considerable scope in the field of security and surveillance: it becomes far easier to create 'pools' of confidential information, computer banks of details available instantly to a variety of interested organizations. And once more the possibility of this has almost imperceptibly pressed towards its realization, government approving (apparently without much discussion) developements which already have their own momentum. This too is a disturbing prospect as far as civil liberties in this country are concerned.

The Industrial Revolution often (understandably) worked on the assumption that if a technique were possible it should be tried: the early nineteenth century was not an age much given to worry about long-term consequences, it seems, and we should not ignore or despise the exhilaration and dynamism of the period. But the growth of ecological concern in our century has shown in retrospect the disastrous results of a 'can = must' approach. What kind of ecological movement might be necessary or possible in the twenty-first century to rectify the possible long-term results of our new 'revolutions' is an uncomfortable question. But so long as technological issues and the discussion of the sort of human beings we want to be are kept so far apart, we shall still be a long way from what the Indian theologian, Metropolitan Paulos Gregorios, has called a 'science for sane societies'.*

As soon as these two areas are brought together, we are at once forced into discussion of needs and Need. And this will be a discussion picking up many of the matters already touched on: the kind of liberty we have and the kind of liberty we need, the sort of mutual and collaborative patterns of life which take 'the other' seriously, the *need* for a model of our use of the material world that is not simply dominating, but allows us to be and feel part of things, not detached and superior to the objects we use (let alone the persons we deal with). A Christian can bring to this discussion the doctrines and images of creation in and by Logos (Word, Wisdom, *tao*); of incarnation, the possibility of full but finite embodiment of Logos; of

* *Science for Sane Societies*, Madras, 1981.

sacrifice, the surrender of assertion, manipulation, self-obsession; and of sacrament, the use of matter to enrich and transform human meaningfulness in relation to the all-embracing order of things.

Furthermore, such a contribution can help to reconstruct the notion of *desire* in the way suggested earlier in this chapter, and so to restore to human life and experience the sense of growth and pilgrimage, the proper suspicion of 'final solutions' and supposed utopias in the historical world – and also of policy based on gratification and passive consumerism. After all, what seems to result from both utopianism and capitalist consumerism is real material privation, both in sections of our own society and in the disadvantaged parts of the world. It may be bad enough that the vision of a video-culture of mass passivity represents a disastrous diminution of imagination and creative intelligence and responsibility; it is worse if we step back to see this static, individualistic and potentially totalitarian society against a global background of increasing economic inequality, over-population in some countries, ageing populations in others, and the spread of military governments in much of the Third World – no unlikely projection for the next thirty years. In that wider perspective, the comfortable consumerism we should like to see, the 'peaceful' society of passive, undemanding gratification at the hands of benevolent technocrats, appears pathetically unstable; and its very character in such a world invites violence and hostility. Peace does not come without *integrity*, wholeness of human desire, which implies the reality of balance and mutuality in the world and so – as suggested already – carries with it the demand for compassion and poverty. In the terms of our second chapter, it involves *contemplation*, which is the way in which the conviction of the non-centrality of my ego finds expression in relation to others, to the material world, and to God. It is, most simply 'purity of heart' in the world of relationships, so that '"they make a whole". "In relation to what?" . . . "In relation to *need*"'.

*

Thus the demand for 'poverty' or simplicity in the lifestyle of the Christian is inseparable from the vocation to peacemaking. The beatitudes are all about 'making a whole' of our world of relationships, in relation to an order of balanced mutuality and growth in and with one another. So campaigning for peace is, in the long run, inseparable from resistance to what I have called 'passive consumerism', to the cheapening and trivializing of desire. And it is in this context, incidentally, that I believe Christian criticisms of pornography should be understood: the question we should ask about alleged pornography is not about its 'explicitness' but about its collusion with neurotic, self-protective and violent fantasy, the various forms of rejection of the world and of the other. Its problem is not eroticism, but that it is not erotic enough – not concerned with desire in its central human significance. And we should also pay attention to the critiques of pornography offered by writers in the women's movement: it is worth noting that at least one such writer* has persuasively interpreted pornography in terms of a fundamental rejection of nature. Women (and other 'inferior' beings such as blacks) have projected onto them a myth of pure 'naturalness', which the male mind both idealizes and struggles to master.

Simplicity, like peace itself, is not a straightforward matter of removing a superfluous top layer to recover a basis of unproblematic goodness. And it is certainly not

* Susan Griffin, *Pornography and Silence*, New York and London, 1981.

a process of exclusion and diminution, boiling down consciousness or culture to a bare minimum. Eliot's famous phrase, 'A condition of complete simplicity, costing not less than everything', is easily misunderstood. Eliot does not say, 'costing a very great deal': we are not talking about reductions at all, but about conversion; not about suffering-in-a-good-cause, but about *death*. The simplicity we have been looking at in this chapter is that integrity of desire, purity of heart, which draws together and takes up the fragments of meaning and longing in us, and, so far from ignoring them or peeling them off, welds them into one act. And that is an act of 'dying' because it involves the final confession of non-self-sufficiency. It is not that we are left with a drastically shrunken self, but that self itself – as we normally think of it – is laid aside: the self as central actor in a satisfying drama, the self as consumer of power-bestowing knowledge, the self as master. It is precisely because suffering is so readily mistaken for death that we see the phenomenon of the person who lives a consciously 'self-sacrificing' life, yet seems fundamentally self-preoccupied – hard or flippant or vain or deeply self-pitying or sentimental: they are all ways of enjoying suffering without facing death.

These are the really shrunken selves. The vigour and assertiveness, the resourceful energy, of the manifestly selfish man or woman are much easier to deal with. But when the basic greed of the ego is stripped down to the morbid self-consciousness of the would-be sacrificial personality, the disease is in fact more clearly visible, the little dramas of gratification more poignant and more destructive.

Simplicity cannot mean this. Its opposite is not rich variety but clutter, fussiness and anxiety. Simple life is life in which we are capable of doing what we do whole-heartedly, which means questioning all those things that cannot be done whole-heartedly because they cannot be seen as parts of a whole 'in relation to need'. I have mentioned some of those aspects of our public life, political and cultural, which invite such questions; obviously the challenge extends to the habits and assumptions of each individual. We need an 'ecological' concern not only for our society and its public behaviour but for our inner life too – an ecology and economy of taste, emotion, sensation. Naturally, this is always in danger of slipping into the disagreeable radical puritanism (and radical pharisaism) which dictates lists of socially-approved habits and leisure activities and so on; and so it is important to keep a slightly sardonic eye on this tendency – remembering the risks of a search for *static* purity or natural innocence and the inevitability of compromises in a compromised society.

Perhaps the things we need to be most alert to (even more, maybe, than to the exact number of commercially produced sausages we eat in a week?) have to do with the response we feel to any invitation from society or the media to easy and unreflective emotions. Mass entertainment often invites us to self-indulgent emotion or easy mockery or satisfaction with cliché. Even the language of 'responsible' journalism often invites the same kind of thing. The great German Marxist critic, Walter Benjamin, wrote in the 1920s that our society was getting to be dominated by the idea of film as the norm of art and communication – the succession of 'shocks', apparently self-contained instants of presentation assaulting your awareness. It is an accurate forecast of what is normally thought of as 'news' today.

So when I speak of 'ecology and economy of taste', I am not recommending any kind of fastidiousness (which would be another form of anxiety). What I have in mind is a degree of discrimination – an active, not a passive, response to communication. Only with a discriminating, questioning response can communication turn into dialogue, and *move*. These are matters touched on a little in the third chapter: the renewal of language we thought about there is in fact one more aspect of our integrity as adult human beings, our simplicity, our willingness to belong to a collaborating and critical whole.

Although it may sound odd to associate the ideas of peace and concentration these last reflections may perhaps suggest why they might belong together. The artist or craftsman at work can show a kind of peace – a lack of restless distractedness and greed for diverting sensation; it is a peace of absorption and self-forgetting, and therefore not a privately-enjoyed sense of repose. It is a peace which is part of response to a given world, engagement and – we may as well say it – love; neither passive nor frantically busy, but committed, and defined by 'need', by the form of the object. Something like this is necessary in the 'art' of significant speech, too. The good confessor, counsellor, or therapist knows that the task is to allow the other to articulate his or her identity and need through one's own attention. You as counsellor are there to learn the inner shape, the grammar, of someone else's mind and imagination so as to enable them to say what they need to say when they see this shape reflected in your presence and response. Again, a peace which is far from passive, but which seeks not to intrude egocentric anxiety upon the world – represented by client or penitent – and where one's own speech and experience are offered not as an imposition but as a gift to the self-interpreting of another. Listening for the *tao*, perhaps.

Sculptors speak of the effort to see what shape is forming itself in the stone, poets of discovering what their language wants to say through them. Odd expressions, but they show very plainly the quality of committed attention we have been considering. And the artist capable of such attention is capable too of embodying it in what is produced – in the balance, the sense of 'inner necessity', which make certain works of art so extraordinary. The contemplative explorations of theme in Bach's 'Cello Suites, the luminous autumnal depth of a Rembrandt portrait, Henry Moore's diverse treatment of the texture of different kinds of stone – these are obvious examples for many. And there are striking failures, too. David Jones is deservedly praised as one of the great letterists and water-colourists of the century, but in a recent exhibition of his work at the Tate Gallery, it was possible to compare the clarity and lucency of many of the early water-colours (especially of coastal scenes) with one or two late canvases, in particular the 'Kensington Mass', where the load of symbolic allusion, barely contained in Jones's poetry, has led to impossible 'overworking' of a surface with detail. A kind of anxiety has taken over, reflective of Jones's tormented mental life: for him, the seeing of endless interlocking patterns of imagery was a positive burden, more and more inhibiting expression. Clarity yields to a desire to say more than can be said – to say, rather than to show?

The Chinese calligrapher, and still more the Zen poet or draughtsman, will wait until the mind is clear and void before executing his work, in rapid and economical strokes. In this way what appears is the fruit of a genuine concentration, a *centring* of the whole person, so that a simple line or phrase can carry and suggest rich content, though not a content to be analysed or conceptualized. This is pre-eminently the art of 'poverty', in the sense intimated in this chapter, because it is an art of contemplation. Nothing could be further from the concentration of furrowed brow and anxious calculation;

perhaps we should do better to talk about a state of *concentratedness*, though even that carries overtones of stressful mental effort. The important thing is that, although it is maintained by discipline, it cannot be described as achievement or possession. It is in fact a further dimension of 'basic trust' – trust that our fragmentariness will indeed be welded into a unity of authentic desire when we yield enough to be addressed and drawn out by the objectivity of the world, both human and non-human. This is not to recommend some euphoric spirituality of pure spontaneity precisely because of the dark struggle involved for all of us in hearing such an address and 'dying' in answer to it. We have only the promise that it is death into the Kingdom – freedom for action in communion; and we have that promise in the realized image of Christian faith, Jesus slaughtered and raised, set loose in the world.

The cost of simplicity is indeed 'everything', nor is it for most of us a price paid once and finally, but an *askesis*, an exercise to be undertaken daily. Undertaken in small personal decisions against resentment, self-indulgence, cheap drama; in continuing discrimination as we look at our society. We can learn to live with *peace* rather than *ease*, uneasy at our social world and its illusions (especially as it works in us), yet un-anxious for our selves and our power. A myth and an ideal, only truly realized in the man we adore as Lord and God precisely because he lived and lives entirely from the still centre of God's wisdom, even when his heart and mind split on the rock of human dread and evasion. But it is that conflict, that collision, which releases the power of the Kingdom, making Jesus the shape and atmosphere of a new world. We enter it in the 'death' of our baptismal promise, and commit ourselves to battle; yet it is in itself a world of active peace because a world defined by those qualities we have been reflecting on: poverty, integrity, compassion.

There is a little fifteenth-century poem which might be taken as a summary of the advance from false peace to true – although its anonymous writer probably meant it to stand for the cyclic nature of human affairs. We go from ease to complacency, to aggressive assertion, defensive struggle, humiliation and – peace; the crucial turning point is perhaps what we do with the humiliation, and whether it can be a real occasion of unselfing. On that depends whether or not the last line simply takes us back to the start again.

> Pees maketh plente;
> Plente maketh pride;
> Pride maketh plee [litigation];
> Plee maketh povert;
> Povert maketh pees.*

---

* No. 136 in *Mediaeval English Lyrics*, ed. R.T. Davies, Faber, London, 1963.

CHAPTER 6

INNOCENCE OR GRACE?

The whole of this book has been devoted to suggesting that peace is a matter more complex and interesting than we might sometimes suppose. We may begin with a simple sense that any systematic programme of killing other human beings is an appalling prospect; we may even begin with simple fear – for ourselves and for those we care for. Then comes the question of how and why such a situation would ever arise, assuming that any sane human being would feel much the same horror and much the same fear.

And here comes the choice between two kinds of reply, a choice which to a large extent will betray what picture of the human world we really have. The first reply is that a situation of mutual military threat arises out of some sort of historical necessity. Technology grows irreversibly, generating new possibilities in the realm of military hardware; and, in a world of competing ideologies and competing ambitions for control, it is essential that it is not only one nation or power bloc that is prepared to explore these new openings. We have to work out what can be done (which means demonstrating what can be made), and even, distasteful as this may be, to project scenarios and construct contingency plans for war. Skill, imagination and unflinching realism in these exercises are essential to preserve peace. We have to show our rivals that we know *exactly* how we should respond to an attack, that we have the material required to respond – and that we know without illusion the full cost, to them and to ourselves. Having a complete nuclear arsenal, making every possible new weapon, constructing precise, comprehensive war games, all this is vital for the avoiding of open conflict. By showing how absolutely seriously we take the prospect of war and how well aware we are of the directions it is likely to take, we and our enemies perform a sort of mutual education service, reminding each other of the price of breaking the peace, and thus gradually pricing war out of the market.

The other reply need not necessarily dismiss all this as dangerous self-deceit (though it may be a little sceptical). Its reply to the question of how we got here will, however, begin further back. Human beings are prone to collective fear and panic, as much as individual disturbance, and one way in which they collectively deal with this is to erect systems which console them by offering comprehensive accounts of their own behaviour and destiny, and whose absolute rightness can be turned into a reproach against all outside. These are – as proposed earlier in this book – designed to guarantee that we do not have to feel guilt for what is done to others. On this basis, it will appear entirely rational to build up systems of mutual threat: the other party is defined from the very start as destructive of our identity, so that we can survive only by threatening his. And because military technology does indeed advance with a sort of pure and unpolitical indifference to both sides, peacekeeping is always a re-adjustment at higher and higher levels. But because this means an inbuilt insecurity running through the whole business, fear and panic are *not* finally contained. They are liable to grow; and since they are not rational things, the likelihood of everyone making rational calculations about the cost of war at every stage is not high.

The first kind of reply in fact assumes two potentially contradictory things. It takes for granted that the situation of deadlock is absolutely 'given', incapable of being resolved – certainly not by any kind of dialogue. This is a deeply pessimistic, even fatalistic, assumption. On the other hand, it argues as if people, especially people in authority, were fundamentally reasonable; it appeals to civilized and enlightened self-interest, and this is a very optimistic calculation, which sets a high estimate on human freedom, human capacity to choose rationally between clear alternatives and to put these choices into effect. Incidentally, the next step in the development of this sort of case is sometimes to claim (despite the expressed doubts of many military and strategic experts who could not by any stretch of the imagination be called irresponsible disarmament fanatics) that a limited ('theatre') nuclear war is feasible: there would be no irresistible impulse to escalation. This is optimistic to a staggering extent. If the basic fact of international politics is a steady undercurrent of will-to-power, it is hardly realistic to suppose that this would amiably give way and one side forbear to use its full military resources in a critical war situation where the other side had a marked advantage.

But be that as it may, it remains strange that there should be such a mixture here of low and high visions of human liberty and rationality. Defenders of this point of view often assert their superior *realism*; but it seems to be a realism which stops short of facing the full consequences of its own assumptions. It says that the world is as it is because of the ingrained fears and prejudices and defensiveness or self-interest of human beings – or as a rule, more accurately, human beings on the other side. But the real calculation to be made is whether or not there could now be a rationally agreed ceiling to the measures governments were prepared to take in defence of their existing power in the world. Recent history is not all that encouraging here; and as the 'balance of terror' is bound to increase irrational fears (and those who govern are not *ex officio* exempted from these), it seems risky to take anything for granted.

The mixture of fatalism and optimism is interesting – and not all that uncommon in immature socio-political mythologies (crude versions of Marxism, for instance). The past is not our fault, and we are not *personally* affected by it at any deep level; it is an external constraint, a brick wall built by nature and history around us. But we are independent and free within these outside walls. By careful, serious, objective reasoning, we can steer our way through the dangerous waters of our given situation. We know the terrible errors of the past too well to repeat them: we inherit the problems of our predecessors, but not their fatal weaknesses. Thus the development of warfare technology (not only nuclear, but chemical and biological) to its extreme possible point can be interpreted as manifesting our superior awareness of the risks we run. Knowing what we know, we are that much more free *not* to give way to violent impulse: we have made quite sure that we and our enemies will make no hasty decisions.

The second approach, in contrast, appears spectacularly pessimistic, and, some would say, far more fatalistic. Here the belief is that the mere possession of weapons pretty well guarantees that they will be used; and that the self-destructive streak in men and women is magnetically compelling. Looking at past history, what grounds could we possibly have for feeling optimistic? We must limit our military resources because if we do not *decide* to do so nothing will prevent them expanding indefinitely. This approach is rather dubious about liberty and rationality; it even seems to want to limit the freedom of states to defend themselves. Does not this suggest just as gloomy and anxiety-generating a picture as the first option?

It may do: belief in the absolute inevitability of war, belief that we are compelled to repeat the errors of the past unless more or less forcibly restrained, is not a humane or constructive view of things, and the cause of peace is not much served by pressing this sort of case. But there is surely an important point here. We inherit limited capacities of judgement; no one begins rational life with a clean slate. Options are restricted by factors beyond our control (defenders of deterrence are right about that), but also our own responses are formed by factors beyond our control. We cannot depend on our – or anybody's – objectivity and clarity; at least, not when the life or death of millions is concerned.

This is not fatalism. It simply points out that there may be disasters which are genuinely *chosen* but not rationally chosen. No mysterious 'historical destiny' forces fingers onto buttons; but all sorts of pressures work on people's minds to persuade them that courses of action are reasonable and defensible. This is so obvious that it seems a waste of time to say it. It is something which affects every area of our lives, and something which philosophers, sociologists and psychologists have alerted us to more and more in the last century or so. The important point is, though, that we recognize (as I suggested in the first chapter) that we are *capable* of irrational, even self-destructive, violence – and it is not something which 'happens' to us, but something we *do*. It is true that we are pushed and moulded by inner and outer compulsions, but that does not make it less our act.

So what is being said is that a great deal of our activity is not as responsible – in the full sense – as we would want to think, although it is not at all unconscious or involuntary. We consciously act unreasonably – i.e. out of fear, anxiety, defensiveness. Now if we are able to use the idea of 'reasonable action' at all, we know what sort of things would count as unreasonable – we know a bit about actions prompted by fear, etc. But, in the case we are discussing, we refuse to raise the question of irrationality. Although we are aware of the human capacity for unreasonable destructiveness, we exempt ourselves – or ourselves as represented by our rulers.

This is where the optimism of military strategists becomes a culpable lack of realism, and our uncritical acceptance of this kind of argument likewise becomes culpable. As I tried to argue earlier, we *must* face the fact that successions of ill-thought-out, short-sighted choices, dictated by evasiveness or selfishness, add up to decisions to accept at least the possibility of total war. And we can hardly suppose that, from a certain point onwards, people will begin to take decisions in a quite different way. All our decision-making as human beings is vulnerable to self-deceit. When we have grasped that, it becomes impossible to believe in the stability of a balance of terror maintained by people who, like ourselves, do not invariably act from calculation and objective analysis. The passion for power can disguise itself in all sorts of ways; what is the next step beyond 'limited' nuclear exchange? And what rationality underlies the calculation, let alone the unthinkable reality, of 'mutual assured destruction'?

We are liable to self-deceit; but part of what we mean by 'rational' living is that we live in communities where our decisions are open to criticism. We reason together with others. In social groups which put a high premium on avoiding self-deceit and remaining open to the truth, the processes of mutual criticism are carefully organized. Not only the international scientific and medical 'communities' (an interesting word to use of them in this context), but the world of the arts also have all built into their lives critical perspectives and procedures – not absolutely water-tight and authoritative, but at least serious in intent.

But somehow the idea of a worldwide *moral* community, in which states may expose their lives and goals for criticism, remains unrealized, despite the valiant efforts and failures of the United Nations. That is why, in the second chapter, I stressed the importance of a Church conscious of its presence on both sides of a national or 'imperial' divide. The very fact of its existence is an invitation to self-criticism. But of course it is far from being the only grouping which thus crosses boundaries, and it is important that there are signs of scientific and medical trans-national organizations also getting involved in a critique of the military rigidities of the states they cover. There are, in fact, embryo 'moral communities' bridging the gulf. In every place where there is a sense of the human vocation as more than a merely national affair, where there is a systematic commitment to truth as a human goal, moral communities are born. If the Christian Church claims to be the most unequivocally comprehensive of such communities, it is not, I hope, out of another variety of power-obsession – but, as we have seen, because of its being constrained by a vision of a comprehensive order of material and spiritual interdependence – a 'doctrine of creation' – and a vision of inclusive or representative humanity as embodied compassion.

The trouble is that a global moral community implies the pervasive possibility of error and of guilt, and if my reading of our situation is right, the one thing our rival power blocs are obsessed with is *innocence*. Governments that assume the givenness of absolute hostility are bound, publicly, to assume that they cannot be criticized morally: the wilful perversity of the Other Side (as we noted in the first chapter) justifies practically anything. And sadly, one side in this confrontation bids fair to make itself institutionally incapable of admitting mistakes: after a brief and astonishing spell of re-assessing recent history and desanctifying Stalin, the Soviet Union seems to have settled back into more traditional patterns of self-congratulation and impregnable self-righteousness. Yet criticism is stirring – even, very faintly, criticism of military policy. The emergence in East Germany of a Christian peace movement which shows every sign of being passionate, independent and courageous is an occasion for great joy and hope. But overall the prospect is still bleak.

If there is a language of mutual questioning that is not threatening, the Christian Church ought to be in a strong position to develop and spread it. Groups of Christians living in diverse kinds of society, under different regimes and ideologies should be, in the first instance, constructively critical of their own societies. They should not be afraid of challenging the 'innocence' of their rulers, because, as Christians, they should have no investment in the myth of innocence. So they are able to show each other that not all criticism is destructive, that they are not afraid of exploratory questioning; and from this basis they can begin to question each other.

This is at present a pretty remote ideal; and efforts to realize it so far have not been promising. The 'Peace Conferences' sponsored by the Soviet Government for religious leaders from other countries have of course never been allowed to raise a critical voice about Soviet policy. Even the World Council of Churches has been painfully hampered by the extremely delicate position of its official Russian Orthodox delegates – and, on some occasions, its moral credibility has suffered in the eyes of many. And it is also true that many dissidents in Eastern Europe regard Western peace movements with deep dismay, seeing the critical activities of Western churches as a sign of the decadence and loss of nerve of non-socialist societies;

some of them see their only hope in a militarily powerful Atlantic Alliance.

Faced with all this, those concerned for peace need to do some hard thinking. It needs to be said, for instance, that military strength is purchased at too high a social – and spiritual – price in our present circumstances. It has to be explained why Western peace movements see justice for dissidents in Russia as inseparable from justice for the world, justice for Third World nations suffering as a result of super-power conflicts, justice, indeed, for the ordinary citizens of the U.S.A. or Western Europe deprived of control over their future and their very survival. Above all, we need to demonstrate the positive nature of our social criticisms. We need to show that our goal genuinely is an enhanced human life.

And this is where all that I have said about the positive dimension of peace and its unity with a humane spirituality comes in. I have argued that we need to be quite clear about the human diminution involved in a nuclear society, but also that we are capable of living out alternative styles of life, rooted in contemplation, receptivity, responsiveness to the Father. If we are to answer the charge of fatalism, we must live creatively, showing that suspicion and the self-critical questioning, even the penitence, that go with it are the doors to a wider vision. The distortions of unexamined selfishness are not simply and instantly done away with, but they are exposed to the steady attrition of self-forgetful discipline, in prayer and in action, combined with self-awareness nurtured by a community in which mutual questioning is possible. And the focus both for contemplation and self-examination is and remains the story of Jesus as incarnating the will and wisdom of God, and thus as embodied truth, transparent to the fundamental reality. Self-criticism does not depend on effort and human invention, it has a given point of reference. Penitence occurs in relation to, in the light of, Christ; suspicion and challenge arise from the clarity and discrimination which should be nourished in contemplation, the silent attention to Christ and his Father which gives us a centre of stillness. Above all, both our self-examination and our silence should open our eyes more and more to the need and pain of others and the reality of the human world's deprivation.

In this way, recognizing that we are already *in* a world of cause and effect and interaction does not in the least imply that we cannot see with some clarity where we are, or that we cannot make some judgements of our motivation. We are not entirely trapped, but we have learned enough realism to know our abiding vulnerability. The revelation of truth in Jesus both establishes our vulnerability – we grasp the force and depth of our self-protectiveness and liability to violence – *and* creates a centre of light against which we may judge ourselves and through which we may grow in discrimination. Thus Jesus is indeed *grace* as well as truth; and the community created by him is characterized by both things.

So instead of a bold but implicitly nonsensical mixture of pessimism and optimism, the Church proposes a sombre realism about our deceitfulness and passionate unreasonableness qualified by trust in the presence of truth within human history. The former vision becomes bearable, we can face it honestly, when (and only when) we are prepared to participate in a community of truthfulness. And that community is in turn bearable because at its centre and permeating its relationships is the conviction that truth can only be shown and spoken in compassion – attention to the other, respect for and delight in the other, and willingness also to receive loving attention in return. If Jesus were not selflessly loving, given up to the Father's creative purpose of fulfilled life for the world, he would not and could not show us truth. His obedience makes him 'transparent'; and because he is 'transparent', he communicates truth.

*

Without the community of grace and truth, charity and clarity, it is hard to see how our individual and collective fears can be dealt with. But of course it is not really enough to talk as though such a community already existed in any and every church group in the world. If we put the problem in these terms, it is plain that we have a great deal of work to do in making the Church more Church-like. What I have written about the Church's possibilities as a place for critical and sympathetic shared exploration among people of differing backgrounds and assumptions looks like either a utopian fantasy or a recommendation of a vaguely religious debating society. Can we see more clearly what sort of possibilities there really are in the Church as it exists?

One of the most striking developments in the Christian world during the last fifteen or twenty years has been the emergence of an international network centred on the French Protestant religious community at Taizé in Burgundy. The word 'Taizé' now means far more than just the original community. Young people in particular, from a wide assortment of nations (and with varying degrees of conventional religious commitment), have come to identify the whole of their lifestyle with reference to what the name represents: a serious political concern, an eagerness to listen and learn across cultural boundaries, a sensitivity for certain kinds of art and liturgy, traditional in inspiration but spare and contemporary in expression, a profoundly contemplative spirituality, an understanding of silence. People have spent longer or shorter periods actually sharing the life of the community at Taizé, or as part of a 'travelling cell' group, going around local groups to animate discussion and keep contacts alive, or in one of the small and fluid groups living among the very poor in Asia, Africa or Latin America. The whole network – it can hardly be adequately described as an organization – illustrates vividly what a critical and loving community might in practice look like.

Of course, there are other aspects. Some (including myself at times) find the luxuriant French abstraction of certain bits of Taizé literature intensely annoying and off-putting. Some have wondered about the nature of the charismatic authority of the Prior, Roger Schutz, and have murmured about 'personality cults' – unfairly, I think, in view of the immense diversification of Taizé-centred activities in recent years, and their relative independence of the place and its personalities. More gravely, the European branches of the network have been stigmatized as dominantly middle-class, even as prone to a slight air of 'bourgeois self-congratulation'. And the abiding romanticism about 'youth' and reliance on the relative rootlessness and independence of student patterns of life (time to travel, lack of obligation to work) have made it very difficult for some who are older and more settled in career or family structures to identify – although again, there have been so many developments and diversifications that it is hard to generalize. But whatever the accuracy of any or all of this, the fact remains that Taizé, and all it represents, *is* a model of some of the sorts of thing for which I have been pleading.

How then does it relate to the ordinary life of the local church – can anything like this become part of our general experience of formal Christian commitment? Certainly there is in the average church a place for the development of groups for shared prayer – not only intercession but silence: perhaps simply making available either a church building or a room in a house for a substantial period during which silence is kept, and allowing people to drop in or out for as long as they need. Likewise, the recovery of an imaginative liturgy will depend quite a lot on the readiness of smaller groups to explore areas of tradition in relation to their needs, in an informal and supportive setting.

But this would become simply a pietistic programme without the reality of education in wider concern. Most people cannot afford unlimited travel or even 'sabbaticals' to experience the life of other cultures and ideologies. Thus it is essential to keep contact alive in other ways – wherever possible, not only by magazines and newsletters but by personal exchange of letters. It is by no means impossible to set up regular correspondence with church groups in other countries; and a periodic exchange of news and thoughts between groups of British Christians and, say, a parish in East Germany or Poland (taking those countries where churches have a little more freedom to manoeuvre) could be an important social witness, even if discussion was not likely to go much further than local gossip. Realism steps in to remind us that freedom to exchange views by letter at any depth is *very* severely restricted on one side, and that correspondents would have to exercise the utmost tact. But at least the practical problems of translation should not be insuperable; if only one person in an area can manage a foreign language, or knows someone who is bilingual, that would be enough.

Well, there is a concrete practical proposal for the beginnings of peacemaking, a serious suggestion for prayer groups or even whole congregations. But any such efforts would be pretty trivial if they had no roots in our own attempts to grow in critical spirituality – poverty, integrity, compassion. And they need too the presence of more large-scale and flexible structures for meeting and exchange, like the Taizé network. Perhaps also they need the stimulus of some quite new kinds of community. Metropolitan Paulos Gregorios concludes his excellent book *The Human Presence** with a proposal for such an experiment.

> There is today an urgent need for an interdisciplinary, intercultural, interreligious community of mature, capable, charismatic people who will live together for five to ten years in a place where, despite the difference of nationalities, they can:
>
> (a) participate fully in the life and struggles of the community around them . . .;
>
> (b) evolve a way of life, a style of living in community, with simplicity and spontaneity, not averse to productive manual labour, not closed to the world outside, not afraid of poverty (preferably in the midst of a non-affluent society), not closed to the religious and cultural sensitivities of others in the community at large;
>
> (c) engage in serious and informed study and reflection on the problems that confront humanity today . . .; such reflection to lead to the creation of patterns of living, producing, and educating which can be copied by the world outside;
>
> (d) embody a new spirituality – *askesis* – based on prayer, meditation, worship, and sacramental life; on loving service and unostentatious self-sacrifice; on humility and graciousness, on overcoming acquisitiveness and aggressiveness; on transparency to each other and to the transcendent.

This is a programme both ambitious and idealistic, and it

* WCC, Geneva, 1978, pp. 100–103.

remains to be seen whether anything similar is likely to be realized. But its importance, as the Metropolitan makes very clear in his further comments, lies in the way in which it integrates the search for an authentic spirituality not only with social and political alertness but with the quest for new technologies and the discussion of values in scientific work – attending to 'need', in its most comprehensive sense. Likewise, it views all these issues as inseparable from the development of small-scale patterns of corporate living in which fears and aggressions can be faced and worked through. If a community or communities like this came into being it would indeed – whatever its interreligious character – be a 'Church-like' phenomenon, suggesting models for the Christian future in particular as well as the human future in general.

A church which could depend upon and look to centres like this would be a far more effectively nourished body than one surviving only on a diet of hopes, statements, vaguely-outlined visions (like this book). The challenge is there; let us hope that there will be Christian people, among others, to take it up.

*

Multilateralists are right: there is always a danger of peace movements and disarmament campaigns becoming narrow and one-sided in their aims. They may castigate their own societies and apologize or even condone the militarism of others. They may reproduce with uncanny accuracy the neuroses of the military establishment, redirected now against governments and allies, instead of enemies. It is, for a British 'disarmer', a real temptation to build up fearful caricatures of the brutality, untrustworthiness and inhumanity of the United States, as vivid as many American (and British) caricatures of the Soviet Union. We have to remember to love our allies as well as our enemies. And they may represent a desperate eagerness to withdraw from the arena of public life, from the real and weary business of creating approximations to justice and understanding between states. They may long for instant and total reconciliation, the immediate dismantling of all our arsenals.

As I have said, I cannot manage to be satisfied with multilateralism. But in all these ways it shows itself alive to morally serious questions. What kind of interim defence systems are being considered? What about obligations to allies and the defence of the weak? What about the whole future of international relations? These are not questions I have the competence to answer – although some have already begun to respond in depth to such queries.* But I have attempted to set the whole issue more firmly in the context of a vision which I hope is at least as wide as that of my multilateralist questioner, the context of a theological and moral picture of human vocation in the created order.

And having said something about the rightness and necessity of large perspectives, let me end with a word about the equal rightness and necessity of small and local perspectives. We can become fascinated, even hypnotized, by the large-scale: the sense of interlocking problems, the huge and *interesting* difficulties and moral complexities of the global view, can mean that no first step is ever taken. We do not yet know or understand enough to act, we cannot predict the consequences. And once again, fear for threatened innocence slips in, disguised as

* The Alternative Defence Commission, established in 1980 by the Lansbury House Trust and the Bradford University School of Peace Studies, is working on detailed questions of strategy. For an outline of possibilities here, see *As Lambs to the Slaughter. The Facts About Nuclear War*, P. Rogers, M. Dando and P. van den Dungen; Arrow Books/ Ecoropa, 1981, pp. 264–7.

exceptional moral sensitivity, if we are not careful. For the Christian, living in grace means willingness to venture on decisions – creative word and deed. We have to trust the worthwhileness of the small gesture and the interim step – signing a petition, forming a group. Or, at the wider level of tactics, we need to press for modest beginnings: it is perfectly possible to be committed to total disarmament (unilateral, multilateral, or what you will) in the longer term, and to see the immediate imperative as campaigning for an arms 'freeze' or an agreement about arms sales or a 'no-first-strike' commitment. All of these are areas of practical common ground between unilateralists and others: the first in particular has unexpectedly united a broad spectrum of opinion in the U.S.A. over the past year and a half. And anything which succeeds in consolidating resistance to the spiral of military development is indispensable, it does not necessarily mean any weakening of concern for the ultimate objective, or rule out other and more radical tactics (the proposed 'peace tax' scheme, for instance) for those more persuaded of the urgency of the situation.

Talking about the limited and local, after all, is not just a matter of practical convenience or injecting enthusiasm into the despairing or apathetic. Christians try to live with the paradox of a limited human story that potentially includes and makes sense of all our stories, and with the regular enacting of a symbol claimed to be abidingly transforming of the world. People who are familiar with the imagery of incarnation and eucharist should not find it impossible to believe in the significance of the local and particular human gesture. Not only is it given meaning – independently of instant visible 'success' – by those central pictures; there is also a trust, obscure but real, that the world's transforming does indeed come and is anticipated in the act of self-commitment involved in incarnation and sacrament, God's self-gift calling out ours. The signature on the petition may be a kind of sacrament, and our own struggle to let peace work in us, in our reactions and relationships, is a witness to incarnation, the reality of transfiguring compassion finding room in the world of terror.

> Christ is our peace. He has reconciled us to God in one body by the cross. We meet in his name and share his peace . . .
>
> Let us offer each other a sign of peace.

POINTS FOR DISCUSSION

Chapter 1

Our own attitudes to violence in the media, or violence in our towns and neighbourhood – how far do these attitudes relate to what we think about war?

How much do we really believe we can make a difference to things – in society in general, in our places of work, in the church?

Are there individuals or groups of people whom we regard as unqualified enemies? How serious is our belief in a common humanity?

Chapter 2

Is it simply idealistic to expect 'repentance' to be part of political life?

Is it right to condemn at international level tactics (threat or terror) we should question at the private level? Or do international affairs demand different standards?

What sort of attitude is involved in 'contemplating' other people? How might the Church explore this and foster it in a community?

Chapter 3

How do we experience language being used by others to mould, or distort, our own reactions (in advertising, in the newspapers, at work, etc.)?

What, if anything, do we ask from people leading the monastic life? Are our expectations of them realistic?

Is it really possible to draw such clear distinctions between privacy and solitude? When we need to be alone, what are we looking for?

Chapter 4

Is it fair to talk about Jesus as a revolutionary? Or – on the opposite side – to talk about Jesus as a pacifist? How do we, and how should we, use the example of Jesus in assessing our contemporary calling?

How do we understand the idea of 'obedience to the will of God'?

In what sort of ways do feelings – positive or negative, happy or painful – affect our faith and trust?

Chapter 5

How are we affected by 'passive consumerism'? How do we react to advertising?

Where *should* decisions about technological developments be taken? Isn't there a case for saying that those with expertise should make the policies?

In what ways is 'need' a matter of more than material necessity or minimum conditions for survival? How should we talk about its spiritual or imaginative side?

Chapter 6

Why are peace movements seen as naïve? What ideas of human nature underlie appeals to 'realism' and are they Christian?

What opportunities are there locally for groups to discuss the question of peace? What practical steps might be taken in educating ourselves and others and widening our horizons?

Are 'symbolic gestures' worthwhile, and if so, why?